THE NEW YORK
PUBLIC LIBRARY
AMAZING
U.S. GEOGRAPHY

THE NEW YORK PUBLIC LIBRARY AMAZING U.S. GEOGRAPHY

A Book of Answers for Kids

Andrea Sutcliffe

John Wiley & Sons, Inc.

Copyright ©2001 by The New York Public Library and The Stonesong Press, Inc. All rights reserved.

Published by John Wiley & Sons, Inc., New York.
Published simultaneously in Canada.

All maps prepared by Netmaps, S.A.
Photo, p.107; courtesy of Andrea Sutcliffe.

Library of Congress Cataloging-in-Publication Data:
Sutcliffe, Andrea
    The New York Public Library amazing US geography : a book of answers for kids / by Andrea Sutcliffe.
        p. cm. — (The New York Public Library books for kids series)
    Includes index.
    Summary: Over three hundred questions and answers provide information about the climate, landforms, people, and places of the United States as a whole and of its different regions and states.
    ISBN 0-471-39294-4 (pbk.)
    1. United States—Geography—Miscellanea—Juvenile literature. [1. United States—Geography—Miscellanea. 2. Questions and answers.] I. Title: Amazing US geography. II. Title. III. Series.

E161.3 .S88   2001
917.3—dc21   2001045403

Printed in the United States of America

10 9 8 7 6 5 4 3 2 1

CONTENTS

INTRODUCTION

What is geography, exactly? To begin with, geography is much more than knowing the name of a state capital or the height of the tallest mountain.

Geography helps us understand the world around us. It not only tells us *where* in the world people and places are, it also helps us see *how* and *why* they got there. Geography describes how places on Earth *change* over time and how humans change the places where they live. Geography also explains the *connections* between people and places. With this knowledge, we can use geography to help us look into the future of our Earth.

This book begins by giving you a geographic snapshot of the United States in relation to the world's other 190 countries. It then takes you on a tour of the 50 states, region by region, from east to west. You'll learn how natural features such as mountain ranges, rivers, and fertile plains have shaped the way the United States has grown and prospered. You'll also learn how the American people have changed the land they live on, for better and for worse.

In addition, this book will help you understand where Americans have moved from and moved to, and why. You'll learn which states and cities are growing, and which are slowing down. You'll also see how we've come to depend on different regions of the country for the food we eat and the products we buy, such as fresh vegetables from California, wheat from Kansas, oil and gas from Texas, and furniture from North Carolina.

The questions and answers in this book are meant to spark your curiosity about the geography of the United States. We hope that by reading this book, you'll soon be asking questions of your own. For the answers, and to learn more about geography in general, we encourage you to visit the New York Public Library or your local library, or perhaps check out the geographic resources on the Internet listed at the back of this book.

PART I

THE UNITED STATES AS A NATION

CHAPTER 1

THE UNITED STATES IN THE WORLD

Where in the world is the United States of America?

The United States is a country on the North American continent in the Western Hemisphere. It is also in the Northern Hemisphere. It is one of 191 independent countries in the world.

Where is the northernmost point of the 50 United States?

It is Point Barrow, Alaska, which lies at 71°23' north latitude (90° north latitude is at the North Pole) and 156°29' west longitude.

Where is the southernmost point of the 50 states?

It is Ka Lae, Hawaii, at 18°55' north latitude and 155°41' west longitude.

How large is the United States in land area compared with other countries in the world?

The United States is the world's fourth-largest country in land area, with 3,678,900 square miles (9,565,140 sq km). The largest country in the world, with 6,592,812 square miles (17,141,311 sq km), is Russia; it is almost twice

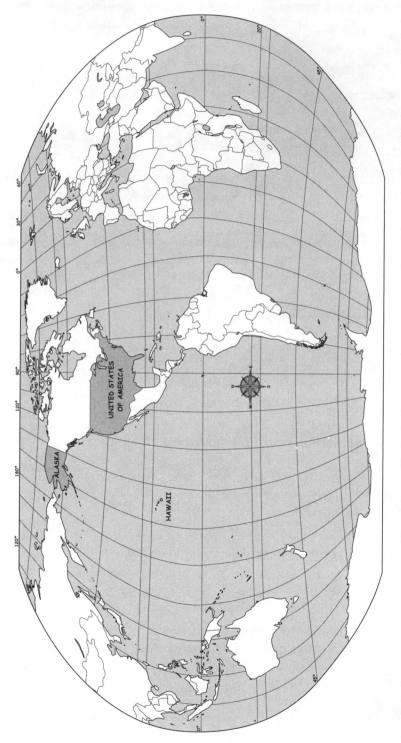

Map of the world. The darker shaded areas indicate the United States.

Geographic Terms to Know

Country: An independent political state or nation and its territories. A country has distinct boundaries, a government, a unique name, and a flag.

Continent: One of the seven principal divisions of land on Earth. The continents are North America, South America, Africa, Europe, Asia, Australia, and Antarctica.

Western Hemisphere: the area occupied by the continents of North and South America and their surrounding waters that lies between 20° west longitude and 160° east longitude.

Northern Hemisphere: the half of the Earth that lies north of the equator, between 0° (the Equator) and 90° north latitude (the North Pole).

Equator: The imaginary line of 0° latitude that lies midway between the North and South Poles.

Prime meridian: The imaginary line denoting 0° longitude that passes through the Royal Observatory at Greenwich, England.

Longitude: The angular distance east or west of the prime meridian, from 0° to 180° east or west.

Latitude: The measure of distance north and south of the Equator, from 0° to 90° north or south. Lines of latitude run east–west and are parallel to each other. Together, lines of latitude and longitude form a grid that lets us pinpoint exact locations on the Earth's surface.

as big as the United States. Canada ranks number two in size (3,831,000 sq mi/9,960,600 sq km), and China is number three (3,691,500 sq mi/9,597,900 sq km). China and the United States are very similar in size.

How many miles wide is the United States?

The distance depends on whether Alaska or Hawaii is included. Measured from the farthest points west and east in the conterminous United States (meaning the 48 states that have a common boundary)—which are West Quoddy Head, Maine, and Point Arena, California—the United States is 2,892 miles (4,656 km) wide.

Measured between the farthest points between the eastern United States and Alaska—Soldier Key, Florida, and Cape Wrangell, Alaska—the distance is 5,503 miles (8,860 km). From Soldier Key, Florida, to Kure Island, Hawaii, the distance is 5,859 miles (9,433 km).

North America showing the borders of the United States with Hawaii as an insert.

How far is it from the southern tip of Texas to the Canadian border?

From southernmost Texas, it is 1,602 miles (2,579 km) due north to the 49th parallel (the 49th degree of latitude that defines part of the U.S.–Canadian border).

Why was the 49th parallel chosen as part of the U.S.–Canadian boundary?

After a great deal of discussion, Great Britain (which governed British Canada until 1931) and the United States finally agreed in 1846 to make the 49th parallel the western part of their boundary. This boundary line starts in Minnesota and extends west to what is now Washington State. There was only one problem: the 49th parallel cuts across the lower half of Vancouver Island. Rather than divide up the island, the United States gave its portion to Canada.

The U.S.–Canadian border is 5,527 miles (8,898 km) long. The U.S.–Mexican border is 1,933 miles (3,112 km) long.

How large is the United States in population compared with the rest of the world?

In 2000, the United States was the world's third-largest nation, with more than 281 million people. China was more than four and a half times larger. Here were the top 10 countries in population at the turn of the century:

1.	China	1.3 billion
2.	India	1 billion
3.	United States	281 million
4.	Indonesia	212 million
5.	Brazil	170 million
6.	Pakistan	150 million
7.	Russia	145 million
8.	Bangladesh	128 million
9.	Japan	126 million
10.	Nigeria	123 million

The United States has almost five times as many people as Great Britain, France, or Italy. It has six times as many people as Canada.

Only 1 of every 20 people in the world today lives in the United States, even though it is the third-largest country in population. That's because most of the world's 191 countries have relatively small populations. But added together, more than 6 billion people live on Earth.

How many babies are born each year in the United States?

More than 4 million babies (about 11,000 a day) are born each year in the United States. That seems like a lot,

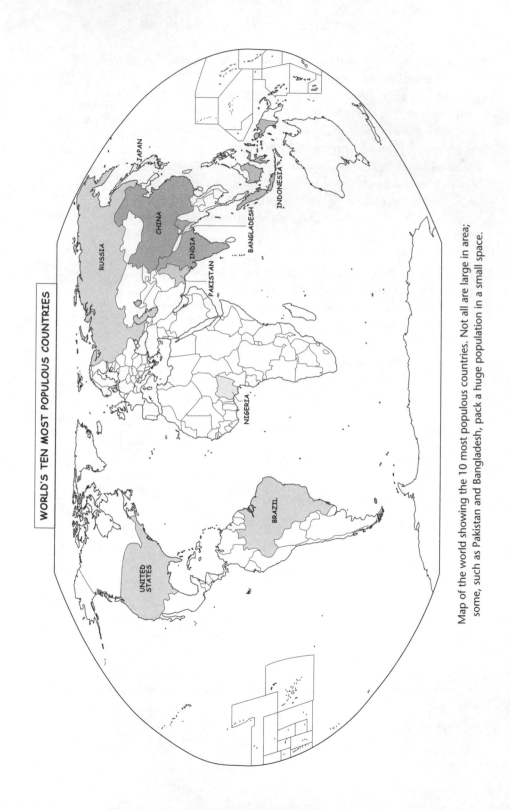

WORLD'S TEN MOST POPULOUS COUNTRIES

Map of the world showing the 10 most populous countries. Not all are large in area; some, such as Pakistan and Bangladesh, pack a huge population in a small space.

until you learn that more than 137 million babies are born in the world each year.

Where do U.S. cities rank in relation to the world's biggest cities?

Just two U.S. cities (in metropolitan area population) were in the world's top 10 cities in size in 2000, according to the United Nations: New York and Los Angeles. (The figures for New York and Los Angeles are smaller here than the U.S. Census Bureau estimates on page 53. This is because different organizations come up with different numbers depending on how they estimate population.)

Largest Cities in the World	
1. Tokyo, Japan	26.4 million
2. Mexico City, Mexico	18.1 million
3. Mumbai (Bombay), India	18.1 million
4. São Paulo, Brazil	17.8 million
5. New York City, United States	16.6 million
6. Lagos, Nigeria	13.4 million
7. Los Angeles, United States	13.1 million
8. Calcutta, India	12.9 million
9. Shanghai, China	12.9 million
10. Buenos Aires, Argentina	12.6 million

The Los Angeles metropolitan area has more people than the countries of Israel, Jordan, and Kuwait combined.

How many people will be living in the United States by 2025?

The U.S. Census Bureau predicts that 338 million people will be living in the United States by 2025—about 57 million more people than in 2000. One reason for this growth is that each year nearly 1 million immigrants come to the United States to live. If it weren't for these immigrants, the U.S. population would eventually start to shrink. That's because American women are having slightly fewer

The first U.S. census was taken in 1790, when the nation's population was just 3.9 million—about as many people as live in South Carolina today.

children than it would take to keep the population at the current level.

Some of the world's countries are not growing at all. For example, Italy and Germany will have fewer people in 2025 than they do today because so many women there are having just one child or no children at all. But there's still a population explosion in the world. Many women in Asian and African countries are having three or more children on average. The fastest-growing region in the world is western Africa—most countries there will double in population by 2025.

What is the population density—the average number of people per square mile—in the United States?

For the United States, the figure is 77 people per square mile. The most densely populated country in the world is Monaco, with more than 55,000 people per square mile. Of course, Monaco is one of the world's smallest countries, at just a little over 0.5 square mile (1.3 sq km). The country where you'd be least likely to have noisy neighbors is Mongolia, which has just four people per square mile.

To calculate population density, divide the number of people in a country into its number of square miles. Remember that the numbers given are averages for the country as a whole, and cities and suburbs have much higher densities. For example, Washington, D.C., has a population density of more than 9,000 people per square mile.

What is the infant mortality rate in the United States?

In the United States, about 7 of every 1,000 babies born alive don't live to be a year old. Although that rate is considered good, it's not as good as in several other countries, mainly because many women in the United States still do not receive adequate healthcare.

Babies born in Iceland have the best chance of making it to age 1—fewer than 3 of every 1,000 babies there die before their first birthday. In Japan the infant mortality rate is not quite 4 of every 1,000. Other nations that have a better infant mortality rate than the United States include the United Kingdom, the Netherlands, Spain, Italy, France, Germany, the Czech Republic, Australia, and Taiwan.

For the world as a whole, the infant mortality rate is 59 babies of every 1,000 born. The worst infant mortality rate in the world is in Angola, where 196 of every 1,000 babies die before their first birthday.

Of the world's 6 billion people, nearly 1 billion cannot read or sign their names.

What is the life expectancy for a child born in the United States today?

Americans born today can expect, on average, to live 77 years. A person born in sub-Saharan Africa today can expect to live only 49 years. People born in Japan can expect to live the longest, to age 80, while people in Iceland, Sweden, and Switzerland will live to age 79, on average.

Is the United States the richest country in the world?

Yes. Economists measure a country's wealth by looking at the value of the goods and services it produces each year. They call this the GNP, which stands for gross national product. The United States had the world's highest GNP by far—nearly $8 trillion in 1998. Japan was second, with $4 trillion, followed by Germany, France, Great Britain, and Italy, in that order.

Of the world's 6 billion people, 1.5 billion live on $1 a day or less.

Another way to measure wealth is to divide a country's GNP by the number of people who live in that country. This is called the gross national product per capita. Using this measure, the world's richest country is Luxembourg, not the United States. The next richest countries are, in order, Switzerland, Norway, Denmark, Japan, and Singapore. The United States ranks seventh.

More money is spent by tourists in the United States than in any other country in the world. Spain, France, Italy, and the United Kingdom, in that order, are the next leading countries for tourism spending.

Does the United States have more working women than any other country?

No. The United States is in sixth place, with about 71 percent of women working for pay. Iceland, Sweden, Norway, Denmark, and Finland all have a higher percentage of women who work for pay.

Does the United States consume more electricity than any other country in the world?

Yes, by far. The United States generates and consumes about one-fourth of all the electricity worldwide. China is second, consuming about one-tenth of the world's electricity, followed by Russia, Japan, Germany, India, and Canada, in that order.

How much electricity in the United States is generated by nuclear power plants?

About one-fifth of electricity generated in the United States comes from nuclear power plants. But most of the electricity we use—about one-half—is made by burning coal. (It's no coincidence that the United States is the world's leading coal producer.) Natural gas and petroleum generate another one-fifth of U.S. electricity, and the rest comes from hydroelectric (dams) and other sources.

The United States operates 104 of the world's 436 nuclear reactors used to generate power. France is second, with 56 reactors. Japan has 53, the United Kingdom has 35, and Russia has 29.

Is the United States one of the world's biggest air polluters?

Yes; in fact, the United States is the world's *leading* air polluter, responsible for one-fourth of all carbon dioxide emissions. Carbon dioxide emissions result from burning fossil fuels, such as gasoline, oil, natural gas, and coal. China is the world's second worst air polluter, accounting for 12 percent of carbon dioxide emissions, followed by Russia, Japan, Indonesia, and India. Most of these emissions result from industrial activity. But automobiles contribute greatly to the amount of carbon dioxide sent into the atmosphere, and America has more cars than any other country in the world.

Does the United States have more paved roads than China?

The United States has nearly 4 million miles (6.4 million km) of roads, most of which are paved. That is more than five and a half times China's 719,000 miles (1.16 million km) of roads. China has about the same amount of land area as the United States.

Do bullet trains, like those in Japan and Europe, run in the United States?

High-speed trains, often called bullet trains, are being planned in several regions of the United States. A high-speed train is defined as one that can run between 150 and 320 miles per hour (242 and 515 km/hr). Amtrak's Acela trains travel at speeds up to 150 miles per hour and are now connecting Boston and Washington, D.C. California hopes to build a high-speed rail system that will have trains running 200 or 300 miles per hour (322 or 483 km/hr). Several other states are considering upgrading existing rail lines so they can offer high-speed train service.

High-speed trains have been running for many years in several European countries; France began its service in 1981. Bullet trains have been operating in Japan since the mid-1960s.

Do people in the United States own more computers and cell phones than people in other countries?

In 2000, a total of 164 million computers were in use in the United States—the largest number in the world. Japan, Germany, Great Britain, France, and Italy, in that order, were the next-largest computer users. The world total was 579 million computers.

Nearly one of every four people in the United States owns a cellular phone. But several other countries top that rate. More than half the people in Finland have cell phones. (Perhaps not surprisingly, one of the world's largest manufacturers of cell phones is Nokia, a Finnish company.) Other countries that surpass the United States in cell phone use include Australia, Austria, Denmark, Israel, Italy, Japan, South Korea, Norway, Portugal, Singapore, and Sweden.

Do most people in the world have telephones in their homes?

No. For example, according to the World Bank, only one of every five people in Russia has a phone line. If you

Almost half of the world's people earn their living on farms or in farm-related activities. But in the United States, fewer than 3 of every 100 people work on farms. Most U.S. farms today are large commercial enterprises that use the latest equipment and technology. As a result, they are highly efficient and productive.

lived there, you'd have to wait an average of five years to get phone service. The wait is even longer in many African, Middle Eastern, and Eastern European countries. Governments and phone companies in these countries are still in the process of expanding phone service, which takes a great deal of time and money.

Does the United States have the most Internet users in the world?

Yes; 4 of every 10 Internet users in the world live in the United States. But if you consider the percentage of a country's population that uses the Internet, the United States ranks fourth, behind Canada, Sweden, and Finland. In 2000, about 280 million people worldwide were using the Internet.

Does the United States sell its farm products to other countries?

Yes. For example, U.S. farmers are the world's leading exporters of corn—in 1999 they sold more than one-fifth of the corn they grew to other countries.

The United States is the world's second-largest exporter of wheat (the countries of the European Union are the first), and it is the third-largest exporter of rice, behind Thailand and Vietnam.

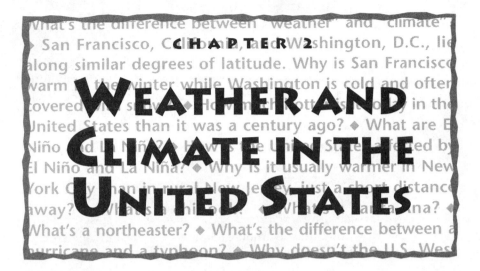

CHAPTER 2

WEATHER AND CLIMATE IN THE UNITED STATES

What's the difference between "weather" and "climate"?

Weather means what's happening in the atmosphere on a day-to-day basis. *Climate* refers to weather conditions that tend to occur in an area over a long period of time.

Climates in the United States vary widely. In fact, they include five of the six world climate groups: tropical (Hawaii and the southernmost part of Florida); mild (much of the South, the southern Midwest, and the Mid-Atlantic); continental (Alaska, the northern Midwest, and the Northeast); dry (the Southwest and much of the West); and high elevations (much of the area of the Rocky Mountains). The only climate category not experienced in the United States is polar.

San Francisco, California, and Washington, D.C., lie along similar degrees of latitude. Why is San Francisco warm in the winter while Washington is cold and often covered with snow?

Latitude is only one factor of several that determine climate. San Francisco's position between 30° and 40° latitude and its location on the western side of the North American continent place it in the climate subcategory called Mediterranean. People living there experience warm, dry summers and mild, wet winters. Washington, D.C.'s, climate, on the other hand, is classified as humid subtropical, a type of climate that is usually found on the eastern sides of continents. Features of this type of climate include hot, humid summers and periods of severe winter cold.

Other factors that influence climate include elevation, topography, and distance from a large body of water. Places at high elevations have cooler temperatures than places at low elevations. High mountains affect climate because they form a barrier that blocks moist air on the windward side from reaching the other side, called the lee side. Winds in the United States generally blow from west to east. For example, Denver, Colorado, has a cool, dry climate because it is on the lee, or eastern, side of the Rocky Mountains.

Global Warming

Global warming refers to the theory that the Earth's atmosphere—specifically, the troposphere or lower atmosphere—is retaining more heat because of an increase in the amount of greenhouse gases. These gases include carbon dioxide (primarily), methane, and nitrous oxide, and together they prevent about 30 percent of the heat that leaves the Earth's surface from escaping into space. The amount of these gases in the atmosphere has increased since the Industrial Revolution began more than 200 years ago. As a result, more heat is retained on Earth, causing temperatures to rise worldwide.

It appears that the amount of carbon dioxide in the atmosphere has increased by 8 percent since the 1970s—the direct result of humans burning fossil fuels such as oil, gas, and coal, which give off large amounts of carbon dioxide. Some scientists predict that rising levels of carbon dioxide in the atmosphere will eventually cause average temperatures to increase by several degrees. If this happens, polar ice would begin to melt, causing ocean levels to rise and threaten coastal cities. Food crops also would be severely affected by temperature change.

But other scientists disagree—they think that the increases in temperature over the past 200 years are part of a natural cycle of temperature change, even though they agree that human activity is increasing the amount of greenhouse gases.

Places that are close to oceans or large lakes tend to get more rain or snow because the water that evaporates from them fills the surrounding air with moisture. For example, coastal areas in Oregon and Washington receive high precipitation because winds filled with moisture that has evaporated from the Pacific Ocean move in from the west and then are blocked by the nearby Cascade Mountains.

How much hotter is it today in the United States than it was a century ago?

Average annual temperatures in the United States have increased by almost 1° Fahrenheit since the late 1800s. Half of that increase occurred in just the past 40 years. In fact, the four warmest years since 1860 all occurred during the 1990s. But it's not getting warmer everywhere; in fact, parts of the southeastern United States are slightly cooler than they were a century ago.

Some scientists predict that average temperatures in the United States may rise by 5° to 10° Fahrenheit over the next hundred years, a change that will affect weather patterns nationwide. One result would be increases in very wet and very dry conditions in different parts of the country.

What are El Niño and La Niña?

El Niño refers to a cycle that occurs every few years in which warm water accumulates in the eastern part of the Pacific Ocean around the equator. Some scientists think this cycle may be caused by changes in trade wind patterns. During an El Niño year, places such as Australia, North America, South America, and Asia experience drastic changes in precipitation, leading to both droughts and flooding. The name El Niño means "the Child" in Spanish and refers to the baby Jesus. Over the past 50 years or so, most El Niño events have begun in December or January, around Christmastime, which celebrates Jesus' birth.

La Niña, which also occurs in regular cycles, results from unusually cold ocean temperatures in the equatorial Pacific. The weather changes it causes are usually opposite from those of El Niño. Neither appears to be related

The word "greenhouse" in greenhouse gases refers to the fact that the environment in a greenhouse is similar to that of the Earth as a whole. A greenhouse's glass or plastic panels serve a purpose similar to the Earth's atmosphere: they let sunlight in and keep the heat inside so that plants can grow.

to global warming; in fact, most scientists believe El Niño and La Niña events have been happening for hundreds of years.

How is the United States affected by El Niño and La Niña?

During an El Niño year in the continental United States, winter temperatures are generally warmer than normal in the North and cooler than normal in the South. During the winter of a La Niña year, the southeastern states generally have warmer winter weather than normal, while the northwestern states are cooler than normal.

Why is it usually warmer in New York City than in rural New Jersey, just a short distance away?

Because cities tend to be warmer than the surrounding countryside. This is known as the urban heat island phenomenon. Cities are warmer in summer and winter because they are full of concrete and asphalt, which retain heat better than soil and fields. Also, heat escapes from apartment and office buildings and warms the outside air.

What's a chinook?

"Chinook" is a term used to describe a type of wind that occurs in the Rocky Mountains. Winds generally blow from west to east across the United States. Chinooks often result when air from the west blows over and down the eastern sides of the Rocky Mountains. These winds can gust up to 100 miles per hour and are very dry and warm—sometimes the temperature rises by 50° or 60° Fahrenheit in less than an hour. Chinook is an American Indian word meaning "snow eater." This type of wind occurs all over the world, but it has different names. In Switzerland, Germany, and Austria, it is called *föhn;* in Italy, it is called *sirocco;* and in Argentina, it is known as *zonda.*

What's a Santa Ana?

Santa Anas are similar to chinooks. These winds blow from Utah and Nevada over the Sierra Nevada mountains and into southern California. The air they bring is very

Winds in Hawaii have their own special names: Kona is a south-westerly wind that interrupts the Hawaiian northeast trade winds. Mauka is a cool, light wind that drops down from the mountains.

dry, which causes vegetation to dehydrate, putting the region at risk for wildfires.

What's a northeaster?

Also called a nor'easter, this type of winter storm blows into North America from the northeast and brings strong winds and precipitation to New England and the Mid-Atlantic states. They occur most often between September and April.

What's the difference between a hurricane and a typhoon?

Both are names for strong tropical cyclones. The regional name for a tropical cyclone that forms in the northwestern Pacific Ocean west of the dateline is *typhoon*. *Hurricane* is the regional name for a tropical cyclone that forms in the Atlantic Ocean, the Gulf of Mexico, the Caribbean Sea, the northeastern Pacific Ocean east of the dateline, or the South Pacific Ocean east of 160° east longitude. In other parts of the world, the terms "severe tropical cyclone" and "severe cyclonic storm" are used. Hurricanes and typhoons are characterized by strong thunderstorms and high winds that move in a counterclockwise direction at speeds of at least 74 miles an hour.

Why doesn't the U.S. West Coast get hit by hurricanes?

Hurricanes form in both the Atlantic and the Pacific Ocean basins, in tropical or subtropical regions. Because hurricanes tend to move toward the west or the northwest, they usually move toward the U.S. East Coast but move away from the U.S. West Coast.

Another reason why hurricanes never strike the U.S. West coast is that water temperatures in the Pacific are much cooler than the Atlantic basin waters. The Atlantic basin is warmed by the Gulf Stream, and hurricanes need warm water to gather and maintain strength.

One western U.S. state that does suffer from hurricane damage periodically is Hawaii, in the North Pacific Ocean. Hurricane Iniki struck the Hawaiian island of Kauai in 1992, causing millions of dollars in damage.

On average, two hurricanes a year cause death and damage on the U.S. mainland, somewhere between Texas and Maine.

In September 1900, the worst natural disaster ever in the United States, the Galveston hurricane, destroyed most of the city of Galveston, Texas. At least 8,000 people were killed in just a few hours.

When is hurricane season in the United States?

Officially, the Atlantic hurricane season runs from June 1 to November 30. But most hurricanes develop between August and October, with the largest number occurring from early to mid-September.

How do Atlantic hurricanes get their names?

When a tropical cyclone reaches a wind speed of 39 miles (63 km) per hour, the World Meteorological Association assigns it a name from one of six lists of names it rotates yearly. If a hurricane is especially deadly or causes extensive damage, its name is "retired" and a new name starting with the same letter is added. For example, there will never be another hurricane named Andrew because of the ferocious hurricane of that name that hit southern Florida in August 1992.

What's the record for the highest wind speed in the United States?

The fastest wind speed on record—not counting tornadoes—in the United States and the world took place on Mount Washington, in New Hampshire, on April 12, 1934. That day, the wind speed was recorded at 231 miles (372 km) per hour. This record is also the world record for wind gusts.

Mount Washington also holds the record for the highest average wind speed over a 24-hour period in the United States: 129 miles (208 km) per hour during that same period, April 11–12, 1934. Mount Washington is known as "Home of the World's Worst Weather." This mountain, New England's highest, lies in the path of three principal storm tracks that cross the northeastern United States. The mountain also has especially steep slopes, which cause winds to increase in speed as they come up from the valleys below. Winds at the summit exceed 75 miles (120 km) per hour an average of 104 days a year.

What is the coldest day on record in the United States?

The coldest day in the United States happened on January 23, 1971, in Prospect Creek, Alaska, when the temperature dipped to –79.8° Fahrenheit. Every U.S. state except one has experienced a day in which the temperature fell below 0° Fahrenheit. The exception is Hawaii, where the lowest temperature on record is 12° Fahrenheit, on May 17, 1979, on the top of Mauna Kea on the island of Hawaii. Occasionally, snow falls on Mauna Kea.

What is the hottest day on record in the United States?

The hottest day on record in the United States happened on July 10, 1918, in Greenland Ranch, California (in Death Valley), when the thermometer reached 134° Fahrenheit. Death Valley is an arid desert basin that covers parts of eastern California and western Nevada.

At one time or another, every U.S. state has recorded a high temperature of 100° Fahrenheit or more.

Does Seattle get more rain than any other U.S. city?

Seattle has a reputation for rainy weather, but it's not the rainiest place in the United States. For example, New Orleans, Louisiana, and Mobile, Alabama, each average more than 61 inches (155 cm) of rain a year, followed by Miami, Florida (56 in/142 cm) and Juneau, Alaska (54 in/137 cm). Seattle receives an average of 37 inches (94 cm) a year.

Even so, weather records show that people in Seattle live under cloudy skies two of every three days, and they receive some form of precipitation 155 days a year. That's a lot, but not as much as people experience in Juneau,

The largest hailstone ever recorded in the United States fell on Coffeyville, Kansas, on September 30, 1970. It was 7.5 inches (19 cm) in diameter and weighed 1.67 pounds (0.75 g).

The wettest place in the United States is on top of Mount Wai'ale'ale, on the island of Kauai, Hawaii, which receives an average of 460 inches (1,168 cm) of rain per year. This location also claims the greatest number of rainy days a year on average: 335 days.

Quick Temperature Changes

The record for the most abrupt temperature change in the United States is held by Spearfish, South Dakota, where it took just 2 minutes to warm up from –4° to 45° Fahrenheit on August 29, 1936.

The U.S. location holding the record for the greatest range of temperatures over a 24-hour period is Browning, Montana, where the mercury went from a low of –56° to a high of 44° Fahrenheit on January 23–24, 1916.

Alaska (220 days a year); Sault Ste. Marie, Michigan (166 days); and Buffalo, New York (169 days). It's just as wet in Burlington, Vermont, and Cleveland, Ohio (155 days), and almost as wet in Pittsburgh, Pennsylvania (153 days), and Portland, Oregon, and Charleston, West Virginia (152 days).

Which U.S. states have suffered the most damage from floods?

In the past 50 years or so, Pennsylvania tops the list of states experiencing extensive damage from flooding, followed by California, Louisiana, Iowa, Texas, and Missouri, in that order.

How many snowstorms hit the United States each winter?

The National Weather Service says that an average of 105 snow-producing storms affect the United States each year. Most last from 2 to 5 days and bring snow to parts of several states.

Does it ever snow in the desert?

Yes—in fact, snow has fallen in almost every part of the United States at one time or another. The most snow ever reported in Phoenix, Arizona, was 1 inch (2.5 cm), an event that has happened there twice—the first time on January 20, 1933, and the second time exactly 4 years later to the day.

Which U.S. city is the sunniest?

Phoenix, Arizona, on average, experiences sunny or partly cloudy skies 81 percent of the days in a year. Following Phoenix as sun capitals are El Paso, Texas (80 percent); Albuquerque, New Mexico (76 percent); Honolulu, Hawaii (74 percent); Sacramento, California (73 percent); Los Angeles and San Diego, California (72 percent); and San Francisco, California (71 percent).

Is Chicago the windiest city in the United States?

Chicago may be called the Windy City, but the nation's windiest city is Cheyenne, Wyoming, where the average annual wind speed clocks in at 12.9 miles (21 km) per hour. Chicago, at 10.4 miles (17 km) per hour, is

The snowiest city in the United States is Sault Ste. Marie, Michigan. It gets an average of 117 inches (297 cm) of snow a year. Second place goes to Juneau, Alaska, with an average of 99 inches (251 cm). Buffalo, New York, is in third place, with 92 inches (234 cm) of snow a year on average.

More than three-fourths of the surface water supply in the western United States comes from melted mountain pack snow.

calm compared to Cheyenne and these other cities, where average winds speeds range from 12.6 miles (20 km) per hour to 11.3 miles (18 km) per hour: Great Falls, Montana; Boston, Massachusetts; Oklahoma City, Oklahoma; Buffalo, New York; Milwaukee, Wisconsin; and Honolulu, Hawaii. The least windy city is Charleston, West Virginia, which has average winds of 5.9 miles (9 km) per hour.

What city has the highest relative humidity on a hot July afternoon?

Los Angeles, California, where the average July afternoon humidity reaches 68 percent. Not much better are runner-ups San Juan, Puerto Rico (67 percent); San Diego, California (66 percent); Juneau, Alaska (66 percent); New Orleans, Louisiana (66 percent); Miami, Florida (63 percent); Mobile, Alabama (62 percent); and Sault Ste. Marie, Michigan (62 percent).

Billion-Dollar Weather Disasters

Since 1980, there have been more than 44 weather-related disasters in which damages and costs have exceeded $1 billion. The worst year was 1998, when seven such disasters took place. Here are the top 10:

1. Drought and heat wave, central and eastern states, 1980: $44 billion, 10,000 deaths
2. Drought and heat wave, central and eastern states, 1988: $56 billion, 7,500 deaths
3. Hurricane Andrew, Florida and Louisiana, 1992: $32.4 billion, 61 deaths
4. Midwestern flooding, 1993: $23.1 billion, 48 deaths
5. Hurricane Hugo, North and South Carolina, Puerto Rico, Virgin Islands, 1989: $12.6 billion, 86 deaths
6. Drought and heat wave, from Texas and Oklahoma eastward to the Carolinas, 1998: $7.5 billion, 200 deaths
7. Hurricane Floyd, North Carolina and other eastern seaboard states, 1999: $6.0 billion, 75 deaths
8. Hurricane Georges, Puerto Rico, Florida Keys, Gulf Coast states, 1998: $5.9 billion, 16 deaths
9. Hurricane Alicia, Texas, 1983: $5.4 billion, 21 deaths
10. Eastern seaboard storm blizzard, 1993: $5.0 billion, 270 deaths

When is tornado season in the United States?

Tornadoes usually form in the spring when thunderstorms create strong vertical wind shears that cause updrafts of wind to rotate at high speeds. This violently rotating column of wind extends from the base of the thunderstorm cloud to the ground. On the ground, the tornado's swirling winds gather up dust and debris, which is why we can see them. Tornadoes can grow to be 6,500 feet (1,981 m) high and 2,000 feet (610 m) across. Wind speeds inside a tornado can reach 370 miles (596 km) per hour.

Although tornadoes can occur at any time, the season of greatest activity begins in the Gulf Coast states in early March. The peak period in the southern Plains is from May to early June. In the northern Plains and upper Midwest, most tornadoes occur in June and July.

The United States experiences more tornadoes than any other country in the world— about 1,000 tornadoes touch down here each year.

What was the fastest tornado ever recorded?

It's difficult to directly measure ground speeds of tornadoes, but scientists managed to determine that a tornado that passed near Bridge Creek, Oklahoma, on May 3, 1999, was traveling at 318 miles (512 km) per hour, the highest winds ever recorded on the Earth's surface.

Where is Tornado Alley?

Tornado Alley generally extends from South Dakota through Kansas and Oklahoma into northern Texas. This area is known for its high average number of tornadoes per year—about 20. But tornadoes can occur in all 50 states. Oklahoma City is hit by more tornadoes than any city in the nation—a total of 103 struck there between 1890 and 1999. One of the worst ever occurred in Oklahoma City in 1999, killing 36 people. If it hadn't been for advance warnings, even more people would have died. That tornado caused $1 billion in damage, the costliest in U.S. history.

How does a tornado in the United States differ from one in Australia?

Most tornadoes—but not all—in the Northern Hemisphere rotate counterclockwise, or cyclonically. Most

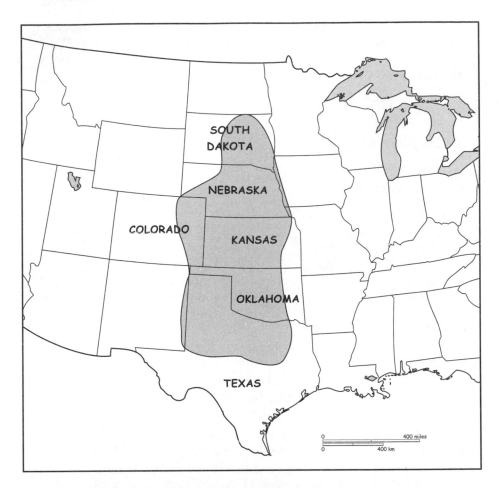

tornadoes in the Southern Hemisphere rotate clockwise, or anticyclonically. Every once in a while, an anticyclonic tornado is seen in the United States (one struck near Sunnyvale, California, in 1998), but usually they take the form of waterspouts—defined as a tornado that occurs over water—like those seen off the southeastern U.S. coast, especially Florida.

Tornadoes are most common in the indicated areas of South Dakota, Nebraska, Colorado, Kansas, Oklahoma, and Texas, an area called Tornado Alley.

What single tornado was the deadliest in U.S. history?

A tornado that rampaged for 219 miles (353 km) through Missouri, Illinois, and Indiana in March 1925 is thought to have killed nearly 700 people. In one town alone—Murphysboro, Illinois—at least 234 people died.

The Ten Deadliest U.S. Tornadoes

Location	Date	Number of Deaths
1. Missouri, Illinois, Indiana	March 18, 1925	695
2. Natchez, Mississippi	May 6, 1840	317
3. St. Louis, Missouri	May 27, 1896	255
4. Tupelo, Mississippi	April 5, 1936	216
5. Gainesville, Georgia	April 6, 1936	203
6. Woodward, Oklahoma	April 9, 1947	181
7. Amite, Louisiana, and Purvis, Mississippi	April 24, 1908	143
8. New Richmond, Wisconsin	June 12, 1899	117
9. Flint, Michigan	June 8, 1953	115
10. Waco, Texas	May 11, 1953	114

The worst multiple tornado outbreak in U.S. history happened on April 3 and 4, 1974, when 147 tornadoes tore through 13 states in the Midwest and the South, killing more than 300 people. The next closest multiple outbreak of tornadoes occurred when 115 tornadoes were spawned in southern Texas by Hurricane Beulah in 1967.

That record still stands for the most fatalities in a single U.S. town or city due to a tornado.

Where in the United States are people most likely to be killed by lightning?

In Florida, where almost 10 people each year—on average—are killed by lightning strikes from thunderstorms. Most of the victims are men, and most are on golf courses. Nearly five people on average are killed each year by lightning in North Carolina and Texas, two other states where golfers and thunderstorms frequently mix.

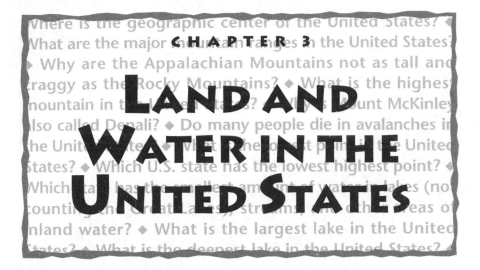

Where is the geographic center of the United States? What are the major mountain ranges in the United States? Why are the Appalachian Mountains not as tall and craggy as the Rocky Mountains? What is the highest mountain in the United States? Why is Mount McKinley also called Denali? Do many people die in avalanches in the United States? What is the lowest point in the United States? Which U.S. state has the lowest highest point? Which state has the smallest amount of water in lakes (not counting the Great Lakes), streams, and other areas of inland water? What is the largest lake in the United States? What is the deepest lake in the United States?

CHAPTER 3

LAND AND WATER IN THE UNITED STATES

Where is the geographic center of the United States?

For the 48 conterminous states, the geographic center is near Lebanon, Kansas. If you take Alaska into account, the center becomes a point near Castle Rock, South Dakota.

What are the major mountain ranges in the United States?

There are five: the Appalachian Mountains in the East; the Rocky Mountains in the Southwest and West, from Colorado to the Canadian border and beyond; the Cascade Mountains in the Pacific Northwest; the Sierra Nevada in the far West; and the Alaska Range, a segment of the Coast Range, in Alaska.

Why are the Appalachian Mountains not as tall and craggy as the Rocky Mountains?

Because they are so much older and have been worn down by weathering and erosion over millions of years. The Appalachians run for about 2,000 miles (3,218 km) from Newfoundland, Canada, through Maine all the way south to central Alabama. They are the oldest mountains in the United States by far, and they are also among the oldest on Earth.

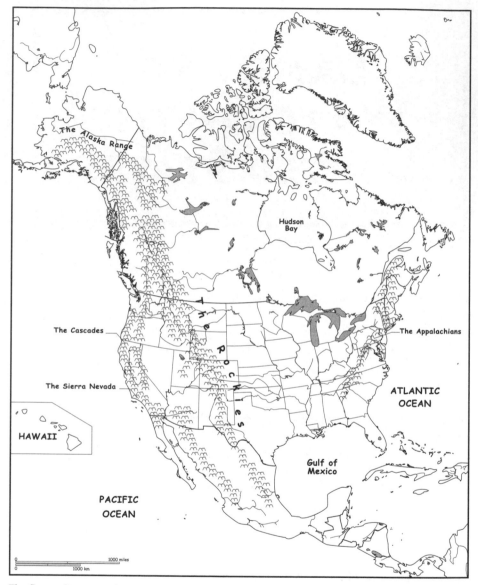

The five major mountain ranges in the U.S. are marked on this map: the Appalachian Mountains, the Rocky Mountains, the Cascade Mountains, the Sierra Nevada, and the Alaska Range.

The Appalachians began to form between 1.1 billion and 540 million years ago. Today, the highest peak in the range is Mount Mitchell in North Carolina, which rises 6,684 feet (2,037 m) above sea level.

The Rocky Mountains in the western United States are much younger. They began to form 65 million to 35 million years ago, and they are taller and craggier than the Appalachians because they haven't been exposed to the effects of weathering for as long. The Rockies run for some 3,000 miles (4,827 km) from Canada to New Mexico, with many peaks exceeding 13,000 feet (4,500 m).

What is the highest mountain in the United States?

Mount McKinley (also called Denali) in Alaska is the highest, at 20,320 feet (6,193 m). On a clear day the peak can be seen from as far as 250 miles (402 km) away. The next 16 highest peaks in the United States also are in Alaska. Number 18 is Mount Whitney in California, at 14,494 feet (4,417 m). The next three highest U.S. mountains are in Colorado—Mount Elbert (14,433 feet/4,400 m), Mount Massive (14,421 feet/4,395 m), and Mount Harvard (14,420 feet/4,395 m).

Why is Mount McKinley also called Denali?

Denali is the ancient Indian name for Mount McKinley, meaning "The Great One" or "The High One." It is in Denali National Park and Preserve, about 130 miles (209 km) north of Anchorage, Alaska. The mountain was renamed for President McKinley in 1896.

The Appalachian Mountain system consists of the White Mountains in New Hampshire; the Green Mountains in Vermont; the Blue Ridge Mountains (from eastern West Virginia to northern Georgia); the Alleghenies (from Pennsylvania through Virginia); and the Cumberland Mountains (from southern West Virginia to northeastern Alabama).

The Appalachian Trail

The Appalachian Trail—often called the A.T.—is a footpath that runs for 2,167 miles (3,488 km) along the crests and through the valleys of the Appalachian Mountains. The trail's northern end is Katahdin, Maine. From there it passes through New Hampshire, Vermont, Massachusetts, Connecticut, New York, New Jersey, Pennsylvania, Maryland, West Virginia, Virginia, Tennessee, and North Carolina, with the southern end of the trail at Springer Mountain in northern Georgia.

Several thousand people each year try to hike the entire route, but only about 3 of every 20 people succeed. Between the time it opened in 1937 and early 2001, nearly 6,000 people reported that they had hiked the entire trail. This number includes section hikers—those who hike a section at a time over a period of years—and through-hikers—those who hike the entire trail in one season. The youngest through-hiker was a 6-year-old boy who accompanied his parents in 1980; it took them 8 months. The oldest through-hiker was 79 years old when he reached his goal in 1998.

Hawaii's Mauna Kea is the tallest mountain in the world—33,480 feet (10,314 m)— if measured from its base on the ocean floor to its peak. Traditionally, though, mountains are measured based on their height above sea level. Mount Everest is the world's tallest mountain above sea level, at 29,035 feet (8,850 m).

Most avalanches are caused by the avalanche victims themselves or by the people they are with. Avalanches are most common when the temperature is between 30° and 40° Fahrenheit.

If you want to climb to the peak, you'll have to try in June because of bad weather conditions the rest of the year. Most climbers take 3 weeks to make the 13,000-foot (4,000-m) ascent to the top from the base camp at 7,300 feet (2,225 m).

Do many people die in avalanches in the United States?

An avalanche is defined as an extremely rapid slide and fall of snow, rocks, and trees. Between 1985 and 1998 a total of 240 people died in avalanches in the United States. The most accidents occurred in Colorado, followed by Alaska, Utah, and Montana. Only a few people died within ski area boundaries—most who died were climbers, snowmobilers, or out-of-bounds and backcountry skiers.

Even if a person buried in an avalanche is able to clear snow from around his face to breathe, in about 15 minutes his breath will cause ice to form in that space—something called an ice mask. Since no air can enter the ice mask, the person will soon die from lack of oxygen, or asphyxiation. Nearly three-fourths of avalanche deaths are due to asphyxiation.

What is the lowest point in the United States?

At 282 feet (85 m) below sea level, the lowest point in the United States is Bad Water, in Death Valley, California.

Which U.S. state has the lowest highest point?

Florida—its highest point is a place in Walton County that is 345 feet (105 m) above sea level. The next flattest state is Delaware, followed by Louisiana.

Which state has the smallest amount of water in lakes (not counting the Great Lakes), streams, and other areas of inland water?

Although surrounded by the Pacific Ocean, the islands that make up the state of Hawaii have a total of only 36 square miles (94 sq km) of inland water. Alaska has the most, with 17,501 square miles (45,502 sq km).

What is the largest lake in the United States?

Lake Superior is the largest freshwater lake in the United States—and in the world as well. It covers an area of 31,800 square miles (82,680 sq km). It is the northernmost of the Great Lakes and touches Wisconsin, Minnesota, and Michigan as well as the Canadian province of Ontario.

What is the deepest lake in the United States?

Oregon's Crater Lake is the deepest, at 1,932 feet (588 m). The lake was formed entirely by rain and snow falling into the collapsed volcanic crater of Mount Mazama, in the Cascade Mountains. Mount Mazama's top fell in about 7,700 years ago. The lake is almost 6 miles (10 km) wide at its widest point.

Do all of the Great Lakes border on Canada?

All but one: Lake Michigan lies entirely within the United States.

Which state borders on most of the Great Lakes?

Michigan borders four of the five Great Lakes: Superior, Michigan, Huron, and Erie. The state of Michigan does not touch Lake Ontario, which is bordered by New York and the province of Ontario, Canada.

Where is the highest waterfall in the United States?

In Yosemite National Park in California. Yosemite Falls is made up of an upper fall, the middle cascades, and a lower fall totaling 2,425 feet (739 m). It is the fifth tallest waterfall in the world—as tall as Chicago's Sears Tower and Paris's Eiffel Tower combined. At times of peak flow, about 144,000 gallons (545,760 l) of water drop over these falls each minute.

What is the longest river in the United States?

The Mississippi River is 2,340 miles (3,767 km) long, making it the longest in the United States. The Missouri River, at 2,315 miles (3,727 km) long, is the second longest, and together they form the fourth-longest river system in the world. The Missouri River begins its journey

The Great Lakes hold about one-fifth of the world's freshwater, covering an area of about 95,000 square miles (247,000 sq km) altogether. If you could empty all the water out of the Great Lakes and spread it equally over the conterminous United States, you'd cover the surface with 10 feet (3 m) of water.

To remember the names of the Great Lakes, think of HOMES—for Huron, Ontario, Michigan, Erie, and Superior.

Yosemite National Park also is home to several other beautiful waterfalls, including Bridalveil, Ribbon, Horsetail, and Sentinel Falls. The park as a whole is about as large as the state of Rhode Island.

in the Rocky Mountains of southwestern Montana, and it joins the Mississippi River a few miles north of St. Louis, Missouri. The Missouri River forms part of the state boundaries of South Dakota, Nebraska, Iowa, Missouri, and Kansas.

The Mississippi and its major tributaries drain a 1.2 million-square-mile (3.1 million-sq-km) area, covering all or part of 31 U.S. states. In some places the river is 1.5 miles (2.4 km) wide. Its source is Lake Itasca in Minnesota, and it empties into the Gulf of Mexico near New Orleans, Louisiana.

Is the Gulf of Mexico part of the Atlantic Ocean?

Yes. By definition, a gulf is a part of a sea or ocean that extends into land. The Caribbean Sea is also part of the Atlantic Ocean.

What is the Continental Divide?

Three times more water from U.S. rivers drains into the Atlantic Ocean than into the Pacific.

The Continental Divide is the top, or crest, of the Rocky Mountains. All streams west of the divide eventually flow into the Pacific Ocean, while all streams east of the divide flow into the Atlantic Ocean or the Gulf of Mexico. The Continental Divide stretches from New Mexico all the way up to Alaska.

Is Niagara Falls in the United States or Canada?

There are actually two falls on the Niagara River— the American Falls in New York State and the Horseshoe Falls in Canada. The Niagara River forms part of the U.S.–Canada border.

The shape and location of Niagara Falls have changed many times over the centuries. Just 700 years ago, for example, there was just one waterfall. The power of its pounding water has, over the years, eroded the rock layers under the river. Today a huge gorge extends 7 miles (11 km) downstream to the town of Lewiston, New York, where the falls first began to flow about 12,000 years ago.

Back then, retreating glaciers caused Lake Erie to spill over, forming the Niagara River. At one location, called the Niagara Escarpment, the river ran over a cliff, eventually cutting through it and forming the falls. The erosion

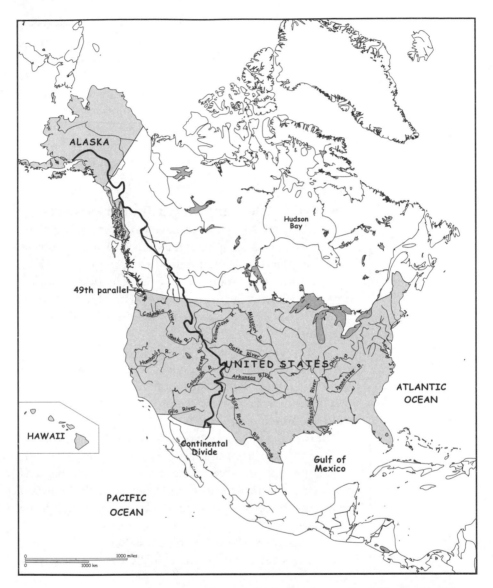

continues today, as the Horseshoe Falls ledge loses 3 inches (8 cm) to 6 feet (183 cm) each year. The American Falls ledge loses only about 1 inch (2.5 cm) per year, because less water flows over those falls.

What is a sinkhole?

Sinkholes are common in humid areas where limestone forms the underlying bedrock. Geologists refer to these areas as karst. Sinkholes are formed when ground-

The Continental Divide is marked on this map with a thick black line. All rivers east of the divide flow toward the Atlantic Ocean or the Gulf of Mexico; all rivers and streams to the west flow to the Pacific Ocean.

water reacts chemically with the limestone and dissolves it over time, causing either a depression or a hole in the ground. Large holes result when the dissolved limestone is part of the roof of a cave. Sinkholes can be shallow depressions of about 3 feet (1 m) or so to straight-sided holes more than 100 feet (30 m) in diameter and more than 150 feet (46 m) deep.

Sinkholes are common and frequently cause property damage in Florida, Texas, Alabama, Missouri, Kentucky, Tennessee, Virginia, and Pennsylvania.

Does every state in the United States have caves?

No; several states do not have caves, including North Dakota, Nebraska, Louisiana, Rhode Island, and Delaware. Most caves in the United States are karst caves. These caves formed when rainwater, which combines with the carbon dioxide in the air and forms a weak acid, seeped into rock cracks and slowly dissolved the rock—usually limestone.

The water that trickles into the caves contains calcium carbonate, or dissolved limestone. When that water evaporates, it leaves behind minerals that form stalactites (which hang from a cave's ceiling) and stalagmites (which build up from a cave's floor).

In Hawaii, a different type of cave—called a laval tube cave—can form from the lava from a volcanic eruption. Sometimes, after the lava on the surface cools and hardens, hot lava continues to flow underneath. If this hot lava drains away, it may leave behind a hollow tube that forms a cave.

Sea caves are formed along coastal cliffs when waves containing sand and gravel eventually carve out holes in the rock.

What is the distance between the United States and Russia at the closest point?

The distance between Cape Dezhnyov, Russia, and Cape Prince of Wales, Alaska—at the narrowest part of the Bering Strait—is 51 miles (82 km). The Bering Strait connects the Bering Sea, which is part of the Pacific Ocean, with the Arctic Ocean, and separates Asia and North America.

Is the Grand Canyon the deepest canyon in the United States?

No; Hells Canyon—formed by the erosive action of the Snake River through the mountains on the Oregon–Idaho border—is more than 8,032 feet (2,448 m) deep at its lowest point and extends for 40 miles (64 km). The Grand Canyon, a gorge in the Colorado River in northwestern Arizona, is more than 6,000 feet (1,829 m) deep in some places. But it is much larger than Hells Canyon, at about 281 miles (452 km) long.

What is the aurora borealis?

Auroras—aurora borealis (northern lights) in the Northern Hemisphere and aurora australis (southern lights) in the Southern Hemisphere—occur when the particles that constantly stream from the sun's surface, called the solar wind, approach the Earth's magnetic field. Some of these particles collide with oxygen and nitrogen atoms in the upper atmosphere, creating a colorful glow in the oval-shaped areas centered over the Earth's geomagnetic North and South Poles.

Where can you see the aurora borealis in the United States?

Alaska is the best place, but people in northern New England may be able to see auroras a few nights a year. Occasionally people in the northern Midwest and the Mid-Atlantic states can see them as well. They are best viewed on clear nights around midnight from September through April.

Why do parts of the United States look like a patchwork quilt when you look out an airplane window?

The regular rectangular farms that define much of the American Midwest and West are a result of a surveying technique called the township method that the federal government required surveyors to use in the Ohio Territory beginning in 1785. The township method continued to be used when the Louisiana Purchase was surveyed in the early 1800s.

A township is a square 6 miles (9.7 km) long on each side, oriented to compass directions. Each township was further divided into 36 one-square-mile (2.6-sq-km) blocks. Every so often, the section lines had to bend to allow for the curvature of the Earth. Later, property lines and often roads followed these rectangles, resulting in a patchwork pattern when viewed from above.

Which of today's states were part of the Louisiana Purchase?

Louisiana, Missouri, Arkansas, Iowa, North Dakota, South Dakota, Nebraska, and Oklahoma were wholly contained in the Louisiana Purchase. In addition, most of the land in Kansas, Colorado, Wyoming, Montana, and Minnesota was part of the Louisiana Purchase.

The French territory of Louisiana stretched northwest from the present state of Louisiana all the way to the Canadian border. The Louisiana Purchase added 828,000 square miles (2.1 million sq km) to the United States in 1803, doubling its size.

How many deserts are there in the United States?

The creosote bush, found in the U.S. southwestern deserts, is the world's oldest living thing. These common desert evergreen plants can survive up to two years without water and live an average of 2,000 years. The oldest creosote bush ever found—at about 12,000 years old—was discovered in the Mojave Desert.

The United States contains four desert regions: the Great Basin Desert, the Sonoran Desert, the Mojave Desert, and the Chihuahuan Desert.

The Great Basin desert covers much of Nevada and spills into parts of Oregon, California, Idaho, and Utah. It is cooler than the other three desert regions and gets some snow in winter.

The Sonoran Desert lies in south-central California and southern Arizona, extending south into Mexico. Some scientists call it the biologically richest desert in the world, thanks to two rainy seasons, in summer and in winter. The tall saguaro (pronounced "swaro") cactus is a commonly seen plant here.

The Mojave Desert is between the Sonoran and the Great Basin Deserts and stretches from California, across the southern part of Nevada, and into the northwestern corner of Arizona. It is the smallest of the U.S. deserts and is home to Death Valley.

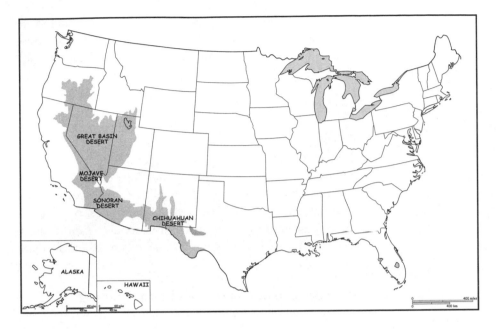

The Chihuahuan Desert is the largest in North America, but only a small part lies in the United States, in New Mexico, Arizona, and Texas; the rest is in northern Mexico. Several mountain ranges stretch through this desert.

Why is the sand so white in White Sands, New Mexico?

The 275-square-mile (715-sq-km) White Sands National Monument, in the northern part of New Mexico's Chihuahuan Desert, is covered with sand made of gypsum crystals, which are usually white. Sand is defined as sediment created by the mechanical and chemical breakdown of rocks. In the United States, most desert and beach sand is made of quartz crystals.

The source of this gypsum sand is limestone from nearby mountains. Over time, rain has dissolved the gypsum out of the limestone and carried it down to the Tularosa Basin's lowest point, the usually dry Lake Lucero lakebed. From there, winds blow the fine gypsum crystals into the desert. No rivers run out of this basin, so the sand becomes trapped there.

The dramatic dunes at White Sands National Monument—the largest gypsum sand dune field in the

The four desert regions of the United States— the Great Basin, the Mojave, the Sonoran, and the Chihuahuan—all have slightly different climates. The Great Basin Desert even gets snow in the winter.

world—are constantly changing and shifting position, a result of the strong winds in the area. Harsh as this environment is, a few plants and animals have adapted to life there.

What's a sand sea?

A sand sea, also called an erg, is a huge area of sand dunes. The largest sand sea in the Western Hemisphere is in central Nebraska. The Nebraska Sand Hills are a 20,000-square-mile (52,000-sq-km) dune field that covers the western third of the state. Because the area receives adequate rainfall, grasses have covered the dunes, preventing them from eroding. Thousands of years ago, sand from a dried inland seabed was blown into this area and formed the dunes.

How do plateaus, mesas, and buttes differ?

A plateau is an elevated area that spreads over a large region. A mesa (from the Spanish word for table) is a plateau that drops steeply off on all sides. A butte is a smaller mesa and is formed when a mesa erodes. If you visit the Four Corners area of the United States—the place where New Mexico, Colorado, Arizona, and Utah meet—you'll see many of these unusual landforms.

How did Badlands National Park in South Dakota get its name?

The word "badlands," to geologists, means a region that has been badly eroded by water and wind. The result is an area of deep gullies and small, steep hills. The soil is poor or nonexistent, and few plants grow there. Badlands National Park in southwestern South Dakota is such a place. It features acres of sharp buttes, pinnacles, and spires of eroded rock. The primary vegetation is grasses—in fact, Badlands is the largest protected mixed grass prairie in the United States.

Because floods and winds have swept away so much of the soil and rock in badlands areas, dinosaur and other kinds of fossils often show up. Badlands National Park is no exception—it is home to the richest Oligocene epoch fossilbed in the world. Fossil remains of ancient horses, sheep, rhinoceroses, and pigs have been found there.

Why does California have so many earthquakes?

Because the San Andreas Fault runs some 800 miles (1,288 km) through the state. The San Andreas Fault is a crack in the Earth's crust that extends 10 miles (161 km) deep in some places. Geologists call it a strike-slip type of fault, meaning the rock on one side of the fault moves sideways in relation to the rock on the other side. Earthquakes can occur along this fault, like those that have caused damage in Los Angeles, San Francisco, and other cities in California.

The San Andreas Fault marks the place where two of the world's major tectonic plates—the North American and the Northern Pacific—meet. When these plates move and collide or slip over or under each other, we sometimes feel that movement as an earthquake.

The Northern Pacific plate is moving northwestward past the North American plate at a rate of 1.6 inches

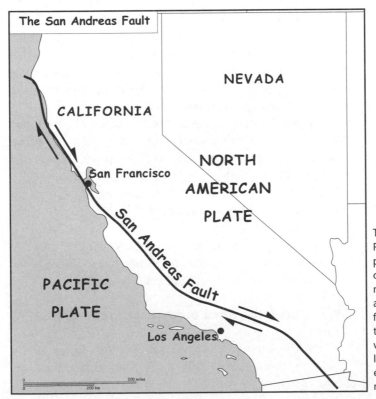

The San Andreas Fault marks the place where two continental plates meet. The plates are moving in different directions, as the arrows show, which causes the large number of earthquakes in the region.

(4 cm) to 2.4 inches (6 cm) per year. At this rate, in 15 million years Los Angeles could become a suburb of San Francisco.

What's a tectonic plate?

The Earth is not a solid shell, but rather slabs of rock that scientists call plates. These plates—seven large plates and several smaller ones—have been moving for millions of years. They hold the ocean floors and the continents. Their movements cause new seafloor to form and earthquakes and volcanoes to occur. Mountain ranges are formed when two plates collide, causing rock to fold and rise. Scientists aren't quite sure what causes the plates to move, but they believe the intense heat of the Earth's core is a factor.

How does the Richter scale work?

The Richter scale measures the magnitude, or size, of an earthquake by using a seismograph to measure the ground motion an earthquake produces. The scale is logarithmic. A measurement of 7 means an earthquake that has 10 times the ground motion of an earthquake that measures 6. We can't feel an earthquake that has a magnitude of less than 2. Magnitude 5 earthquakes begin to cause real damage. The scale has no top number.

Another way to measure earthquakes is the modified Mercalli scale, which measures the intensity of an earthquake based on observations of the physical damage done. It uses Roman numerals I through XII, in which I means no damage, VI means slight damage, and XII means total damage, with no structures left standing and objects thrown into the air.

A third way to measure earthquakes is the moment magnitude scale, which uses a seismogram to measure the movement of the Earth's surface during the quake.

What's been the worst earthquake in the United States?

On the Richter scale, Alaska's Good Friday earthquake in 1964 in Prince William Sound measured 9.2, the strongest ever recorded. This quake was felt over a

500,000-square-mile (1.3 million–sq-km) area, killed 114 people, and released more than 125 times the energy of the San Francisco earthquake of April 18, 1906. But in terms of loss of life and property damage, the 1906 San Francisco earthquake was the most devastating. It claimed 700 lives and caused millions of dollars of damage, much of it caused by the fires that followed. Scientists at the U.S. Geological Survey estimate that it had a magnitude of 7.7 on the Richter scale; people hundreds of miles away felt it.

Can earthquakes be predicted?

No, not to date. Geologists can, however, calculate the probability of future earthquakes based on past activity. They know that very large earthquakes have happened along the southern part of the San Andreas Fault about every 150 years for the past 1,500 years or so.

A large quake hit that area in 1857, so they believe another may be due there in the next several decades. Some have estimated the probability of a major earthquake in San Francisco at 67 percent over the next 30 years.

Ten Strongest Earthquakes in the United States		
Location	Date	Richter Scale Magnitude
1. Prince William Sound, Alaska	March 28, 1964	9.2
2. Andreanof Islands, Alaska	March 9, 1957	8.8
3. Rat Islands, Alaska	February 4, 1965	8.7
4. (tie) East of Shumagin Islands, Alaska	November 10, 1938	8.3
Lituya Bay, Alaska	July 10, 1958	8.3
6. (tie) Yakutat Bay, Alaska	September 10, 1899	8.2
Near Cape Yakataga, Alaska	September 4, 1899	8.2
8. Andreanof Islands, Alaska	May 7, 1986	8.0
9. (tie) New Madrid, Missouri	February 7, 1812	7.9
Fort Tejon, California	January 9, 1857	7.9

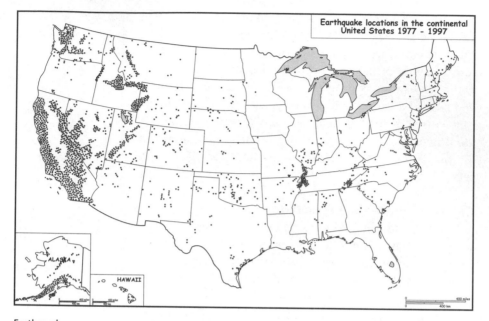

Earthquake locations in the continental
United States 1977 - 1997

Earthquakes can occur almost anywhere in the United States, but as this map shows, most occur on the West Coast and in Alaska.

What's a tsunami? Do they occur in the United States?

Tsunami are huge, destructive waves that follow an earthquake or disturbance that has happened in the Earth's crust under the ocean. The word is Japanese, meaning harbor wave; it's pronounced "tsoo-nah-mee." They're wrongly called tidal waves, since they have nothing to do with the tides. During an earthquake, cracks open up along the ocean floor. When water rushes into the hole and then bounces back out onto the surface, it causes strong swells to form, which can travel over open ocean up to 400 or 500 miles (644 or 800 km) per hour. When these swells reach the shallow waters near a coastline, they are slowed down by friction from the seabed. Then they are transformed into very high waves, averaging 30 feet (9 m) high and often much higher.

Once ashore, these huge waves can crush structures along the coastline and cause immense flooding. Most tsunami occur in the Pacific Ocean. Tsunami have hit the United States in Alaska and Hawaii.

Does the United States have any active volcanoes?

Yes. In fact, the United States is third in the world in the number of active volcanoes ever recorded, behind

Earthquakes in Missouri

Even though most U.S. earthquakes happen in California and Alaska, earthquakes have been recorded in every U.S. state. The fewest occur in Florida and North Dakota. The largest earthquake in the conterminous United States (i.e., excluding Alaska and Hawaii) happened on February 7, 1812, along the New Madrid Fault at New Madrid in southeastern Missouri (at the point where Kentucky and Tennessee border Missouri, along the Mississippi River). Its magnitude has been estimated at 7.9 (although some geologists have estimated as much as 8.7) on the Richter scale.

Two other very large earthquakes were recorded along the same fault just one and two months earlier—in December 1811 and in January 1812. Luckily, only about 400 people lived in the area at that time, but the effects were felt for hundreds of miles. Some accounts claimed the quake caused church bells to ring in Boston, Massachusetts!

Geologists predict that there is a 90 percent probability that the New Madrid Fault will produce a magnitude 6 or 7 earthquake within the next 50 years. Millions of people living in the Mississippi Valley area, including those in Memphis, Tennessee, and St. Louis, Missouri, would be affected.

Indonesia and Japan. About 1,500 volcanoes have erupted all over the world in the past 10,000 years, and about 150 of those were in the United States. Today, active volcanoes are found in Hawaii, Washington, Oregon, California, and Alaska.

Hawaii is home to six active volcanoes. Mauna Loa has erupted 15 times since 1900 and is one of the world's largest active volcanoes. Kilauea is one of the world's most active volcanoes and has been erupting continuously since 1983. (See more about Hawaiian volcanoes on page 138.)

Volcanoes in the Cascade range in California, Oregon, and Washington are less active but potentially more dangerous because so many people live nearby. Active volcanoes in Washington are Mount Baker, which last showed signs of activity in 1976; Mount Rainier, which has been quiet for the past 500 years; and Mount St. Helens, which erupted in 1980 and caused enormous destruction. (See more about Mount Rainier and Mount St. Helens on pages 144–145) Lassen Peak in California erupted between 1914 and 1917.

About 80 volcanic centers, each with one or more volcanoes, exist in the Alaska peninsula and the Aleutian Islands. On average, about one or two eruptions occur each year there. One of those volcanoes, Novarupta, on the Alaska Peninsula, erupted in 1912 and spewed out 30 times the volume of magma produced by Mount St. Helens in 1980. The volcano was the world's largest in the twentieth century.

CHAPTER 4

PEOPLE AND PLACES IN THE UNITED STATES

How many people live in the United States?

The 2000 Census showed that about 281 million people lived in the United States, excluding Puerto Rico and the U.S. island territories. The U.S. Census Bureau's Web page features a population clock that shows the estimated U.S. population as it changes daily; go to the www.census.gov site to see the current population.

What are the 10 largest states in population?

The 10 largest U.S. states as of the 2000 Census were:

1.	California	33,871,648
2.	Texas	20,851,820
3.	New York	18,976,457
4.	Florida	15,982,378
5.	Illinois	12,419,293
6.	Pennsylvania	12,281,054
7.	Ohio	11,353,140
8.	Michigan	9,938,444
9.	New Jersey	8,414,350
10.	Georgia	8,186,453

U.S. Census Bureau experts predict that by 2025, Florida will become the third-largest state, bumping New York to the fourth spot.

More than twice as many people live in Detroit, Michigan, as live in the entire state of Wyoming. More people live in the Phoenix, Arizona, metropolitan area than live in the entire state of Oregon. And, strangely enough, more people live in the New York City metropolitan area—because it includes parts of surrounding states—than live in the entire state of New York.

How many people will be living in the United States a hundred years from now?

More than twice as many as in 2000, says the Census Bureau. Experts predict that the nation will have 338 million people by 2025, 404 million people by 2050, and 571 million by 2100. They expect this increase even though the U.S. birthrate is stable, at about two children per woman on average.

Then why so much growth? Because in the years ahead, the number of women of childbearing age will increase. As a result, more children will be born, in total, than are being born today. In addition, people will continue to move to the United States from other countries.

Which states are growing the fastest?

The western states are growing in population much faster than the United States as a whole. Colorado, Idaho, Nevada, and Arizona each grew by more than 30 percent during the 1990s, while the total U.S. growth rate was 13 percent. Nevada grew by more than 66 percent, the fastest-growing state of all. Other fast-growing western states were Washington, Oregon, and Utah. Several south-

The fastest growing U.S. states are in the South and the West.

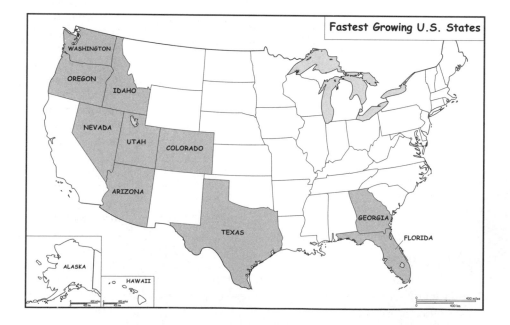

Fastest Growing U.S. States

ern states also are growing at a rapid rate, especially Texas, Florida, and Georgia.

The slowest-growing states during the 1990s were North Dakota, West Virginia, Pennsylvania, Connecticut, and Maine.

Florida's population today is six times larger than it was in 1950.

Is Puerto Rico part of the United States?

Yes. Puerto Rico, an island in the Caribbean Sea southeast of Florida, is a U.S. territory, with 3.8 million people. Puerto Rico became a U.S. territory, along with the Pacific island of Guam, when the Treaty of Paris was signed after the Spanish-American War in 1898. Puerto Rico became a commonwealth in 1952, meaning that it governs itself under its own constitution.

Several efforts to gain U.S. statehood for Puerto Rico were defeated when they were put to popular vote in the 1990s. Many of its citizens would like the island to be an independent nation. Puerto Ricans are U.S. citizens, but they do not have to pay federal income taxes. They send a resident commissioner to speak for them in the U.S. House of Representatives, but this person may vote only in congressional committees.

Are the Virgin Islands also part of the United States?

Yes. The U.S. Virgin Islands (not to be confused with the British Virgin Islands) are a territory of the United States. They lie about 40 miles (64 km) east of Puerto Rico. The U.S. government purchased this group of 50 islands and cays from Denmark in 1917. The reason? During World War I, the U.S. government wanted to be able to control this strategic spot in the Caribbean.

Other U.S. territories include the Northern Mariana Islands, American Samoa, Guam, the Midway Islands, and several other Pacific Ocean islands, most of which were important to the U.S. military in World War II.

People living in U.S. territories are U.S. citizens, and each territory may have one nonvoting delegate in the U.S. House of Representatives.

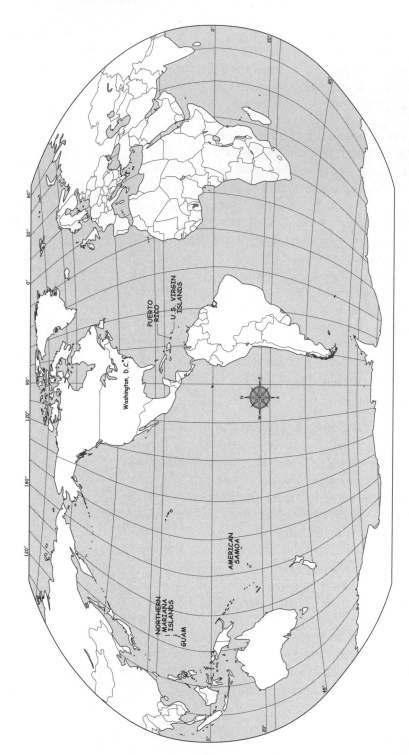

The United States has very small territories, but they are widely scattered, as this map makes clear. Some, such as Puerto Rico and the U.S. Virgin Islands, are in the Caribbean, close to the mainland; others, such as Guam and American Samoa, are quite distant, far away in the Pacific Ocean.

Do African Americans make up the largest minority group in the United States?

Yes, but Hispanics are not far behind. In 2000, African Americans made up 12.8 percent of the U.S. population, while Hispanics represented 12.5 percent, Asians and Pacific Islanders about 4.1 percent; and Native Americans 0.9 percent.

By 2015, the U.S. Census Bureau predicts, Hispanics will make up about 15.8 percent of the U.S. population and become the largest minority group. By that time the percentage of African Americans will have grown to 13.6 percent, while Asians and Pacific Islanders will form about 5.6 percent of the total population. The number of Native Americans will increase slightly, to form 1 percent of the U.S. population.

Today, minority groups are not really in the minority in California, Hawaii, New Mexico, and the District of Columbia, where they make up more than half of the population. And almost half (46 percent) of the people living in Texas are minority group members.

How many people come from other countries to live in the United States each year?

Almost a million people immigrate to the United States yearly, although the Census Bureau predicts that the number will drop to about 700,000 a year by 2010. The main reason people come to the United States is for better-paying jobs. For example, one study showed that people who were earning only about $31 a week in Mexico could make $278 a week in the United States.

How many people living in the United States were born in other countries?

About 26 million of the 273 million people living in the United States in 1999 were born somewhere else. Half were born in Latin America, including Mexico, Cuba, the Dominican Republic, and El Salvador. A fourth were born in Asia, including the Philippines, China, Vietnam, and India. A fifth were born in Europe.

Half of all foreign-born people in the United States live in these five metropolitan areas: Los Angeles, New York, Miami, San Francisco, and Chicago.

How many people visit the United States from other countries each year?

Nearly 50 million people visit the United States from other countries each year. Most of them are tourists or

The Trail of Tears

Americans have been a people on the move since the nation's beginnings. But as European settlers moved in, Native Americans lost out. The population of Native Americans was between 5 million and 10 million when English colonists first landed in the 1600s, but by 1900 fewer than 250,000 Native Americans were left. Many died from disease—they had little immunity to European infections—and in fights with settlers.

In the late 1830s, the U.S. government moved about 17,000 Cherokees from their homelands in the southeastern United States to the Indian Territory, in what is now Oklahoma. The road they traveled became known as the Trail of Tears because 4,000 died while making the journey. Today the National Park Service administers the Trail of Tears National Historic Trail.

businesspeople, and most come from Canada and Europe. Interestingly, in recent years more Europeans visited the United States than the number of Americans who visited Europe.

How many people living in the United States don't speak English as their first language?

More than 30 million Americans are nonnative speakers of English. Spanish-speaking people lead the list, followed by native speakers of French, German, Italian, Chinese, Tagalog, Polish, Korean, and Vietnamese.

What's the difference between a city and a metropolitan area?

A metropolitan area is much larger than the area within the official city limits. A metropolitan area includes the central core city as well as the nearby communities that are tied to that city in terms of business and social activities. The U.S. Census Bureau defines these metropolitan areas. Here are their population estimates for the nation's largest metropolitan areas as of mid-1999:

Twenty Largest U.S. Metropolitan Areas

1. New York–northern New Jersey– southwestern Connecticut– Long Island   20,196,649
2. Los Angeles-Riverside-Orange County   16,036,587
3. Chicago-Gary-Kenosha   8,885,919
4. Washington, D.C.–Baltimore   7,359,044
5. San Francisco–Oakland–San Jose   6,873,645
6. Philadelphia–Wilmington–Atlantic City   5,999,034
7. Boston–Worcester–Lawrence   5,667,225
8. Detroit–Ann Arbor–Flint   5,469,312
9. Dallas–Fort Worth   4,909,523
10. Houston–Galveston–Brazoria   4,493,741
11. Atlanta   3,857,097
12. Miami–Fort Lauderdale   3,711,102
13. Seattle–Tacoma–Bremerton   3,465,760
14. Phoenix–Mesa   3,013,696
15. Cleveland–Akron   2,910,616
16. Minneapolis–St. Paul   2,872,109
17. San Diego   2,820,844
18. St. Louis   2,569,029
19. Denver–Boulder–Greeley   2,417,908
20. Pittsburgh   2,331,336

The following table lists the 10 largest U.S. cities if you consider only the number of people living within the official city limits. Notice that after the top three, the city rankings are quite different from the previous list.

1. New York   7,428,162
2. Los Angeles   3,633,591
3. Chicago   2,799,050

In land area, Juneau, Alaska, is larger than the entire state of Delaware. The city limits of Juneau encompass 3,081 square miles (8,011 sq km), while Delaware has 2,057 square miles (5,348 sq km). Here's another comparison: the city of San Antonio, Texas, is 400 square miles (1,040 sq km), making it larger in area than New York City, which has 309 square miles (803 sq km).

4. Houston	1,845,967
5. Philadelphia	1,417,601
6. San Diego	1,238,974
7. Phoenix	1,211,466
8. San Antonio	1,147,213
9. Dallas	1,076,214
10. Detroit	965,084

Which U.S. metropolitan areas grew the fastest in the 1990s?

All of the fastest-growing cities were in the West or the South. Number one is Las Vegas, which added nearly half a million residents to its population between 1990 and 1998. Following Las Vegas, in order, are Laredo, Texas; McAllen–Edinburg–Mission, Texas; Boise City, Idaho; Naples, Florida; Phoenix–Mesa, Arizona; Austin–San Marcos, Texas; Fayetteville–Springdale–Rogers, Arkansas; Wilmington, North Carolina; and Provo–Orem, Utah.

Which metropolitan areas have been losing people?

Most are in the North or East: the areas shrinking fastest in the 1990s were Utica–Rome, New York; Binghamton, New York; Steubenville–Weirton, Ohio–West Virginia; and Grand Forks, North Dakota–Minnesota.

More than half of the people in the United States live within 50 miles (80 km) of a coastline.

Which state has the most miles of coastline?

Alaska has the most, but Michigan—not Florida or California, as you might think—comes in second, because of its 3,288-mile (5,290-km) shoreline along the Great Lakes.

What's a megalopolis?

"Megalopolis" is a word that originally referred to the largely urban East Coast area that spreads from Boston to Washington, D.C. But now it means any multicity urban area of more that 10 million people.

What's an edge city?

An edge city is a booming suburban area that has sprung up since the 1970s, usually near a major highway. It contains many large office buildings and shopping centers but not very many homes and apartments. An example is Tysons Corner, Virginia, next to the Capital Beltway (I-495) a few miles from Washington, D.C.

What is urban sprawl?

Urban sprawl refers to the spread of suburban housing developments that extend far beyond the city where most people work. When an urban area spreads, traffic problems increase and the city's downtown area begins to decay, as shops and restaurants move to the suburbs. The Sierra Club says that Los Angeles, San Diego, and Phoenix are the worst cities for urban sprawl in the United States. It also says that Atlanta, St. Louis, Washington, D.C., and Cincinnati are the most sprawl-threatened large cities.

What's the difference between a town and a city?

A town is often defined as having between 2,500 and 20,000 residents, but there are no strict guidelines.

Which state has the most children under age 18? Which state has the fewest?

Utah tops the list, with a third of the total population under age 18, followed by Alaska and New Mexico. West Virginia has the fewest, where only one of every five people is under age 18. About 70 percent of the people who live in Utah are Mormons, who tend to have large families.

How many people move from one place to another in the United States each year?

In 1998, about 16 percent of the U.S. population—forty-three million people—changed addresses. Most moved within their own county, but 15 percent packed up and moved to another state.

The most common name for a city or town in the United States is Midway, with 180 so named. The next most popular names are Fairview (163) and Oak Grove (125).

*The average
American
changes residence
11 to 13 times
over a lifetime.*

Where are the riskiest places to live in the United States?

If you want to avoid earthquakes, landslides, wildfires, and volcanoes, don't live in California, according to geographer Mark Monmonier. Other risky places to live include Seattle, Washington, with its nearby active volcanoes and vulnerability to earthquakes. Coastal areas of Hawaii and Alaska are unsafe because of possible tsunamis (see page 44 for more about these). The southern United States can be dangerous because of hurricanes and flooding, in particular North Carolina's Outer Banks; Miami, Florida; and the Louisiana coast.

Which state has the highest percentage of students graduating from high school?

In Alaska, 9 of 10 high school students get their diplomas. The lowest percentage of graduates is in South Carolina, where only three of four students finish high school. The 10 states with the lowest rankings in high school completion were southern states or states that bordered on southern states.

What are the most common surnames in the United States?

In order, they are Smith, Johnson, Williams, Jones, and Brown.

What is the largest church group in the United States?

By far, the Roman Catholic Church, which has 62 million members in the United States. Next in line are the Southern Baptist Convention, with 15.7 million; the United Methodist Church, with 8.4 million; the National Baptist Convention USA, Inc., with 8.2 million; the Church of God in Christ, with 5.5 million; and the Evangelical Lutheran Church in America, 5.2 million.

By region, Catholics tend to live in the Northeast, Southwest, and West. Baptists tend to live in the South, especially in Mississippi, Alabama, and Georgia. States having the most Methodists include Delaware, Iowa, South

Carolina, West Virginia, and Kansas. Large numbers of Lutherans live in North Dakota, South Dakota, Minnesota, Wisconsin, and Nebraska.

There are about 4.3 million Jews in the United States, making up about 2 percent of the population.

An estimated 4 million to 6 million Muslims (people who practice the Islamic religion) now live in the United States, and the number is growing steadily. Although Muslims have lived in the United States since its beginnings, many more immigrated to the United States after a change in immigration laws in 1965, which allowed immigrants who could make an immediate and substantial contribution to society, such as doctors and engineers, to move here. After that time, many professional people came to the United States from largely Islamic countries such as Pakistan, Bangladesh, and several Arabian countries. After Christianity, Islam is the second-largest religious group in the world, with more than a billion practitioners worldwide.

What's the most common street name in the United States?

If you guessed Main Street, you'd be wrong. It's Second Street, mainly because many former Main Streets and First Streets were later given other names. In second place is Park Street, followed by Third, Fourth, and Fifth Streets. The most popular street name with a proper name is Washington Street.

What's the longest bridge in the United States?

The longest bridge in America is also the longest over-water bridge in the world: the 24-mile (38-km)-long Lake Pontchartrain Causeway near New Orleans, Louisiana.

The Verrazano–Narrows Bridge in New York City is the longest suspension bridge in the United States, with a span of 4,260 feet (1,298 m). Close behind is San Francisco's Golden Gate Bridge, with a span of 4,200 feet (1,219 m). Those two bridges are the sixth and seventh-longest suspension bridges in the world; Japan, Denmark,

Before the transcontinental railroad was built, a trip across the United States took 4 to 6 months. Taking the train reduced coast-to-coast travel time to 6 days. Today, airplanes routinely make the trip nonstop in under five hours if the plane is flying from the West Coast to the East Coast, and in about 6 hours if the plane is flying from the East Coast to the West Coast. It takes longer to fly from east to west because the plane has to fly into prevailing winds. Winds in the United States generally are westerly, meaning they blow from west to east.

England, and China have longer ones. The Mackinac Straits suspension bridge in Michigan is the ninth-longest suspension bridge in the world and the third-longest in the United States, at 3,800 feet (1,158 m).

Where did the two rails of the nation's first transcontinental railroad begin and end?

From the west, the Central Pacific Railroad began building track in Sacramento, California. From the east, the Union Pacific began construction in Omaha, Nebraska. (Railroads running from the East Coast to Omaha had already been built.) It took about six years of backbreaking labor until the two tracks met at Promontory Point, Utah, in 1869. Most of the workers were immigrants—Irish for the Union Pacific and Chinese for the Central Pacific. These workers laid as many as 10 miles (16 km) of track a day, without using heavy machinery.

Why was the U.S. Interstate Highway system built?

In the 1950s, President Dwight D. Eisenhower saw the need for the United States to have sufficient evacuation

The first transcontinental railroad stretched from Omaha, Nebraska, to Sacramento, California; the black-and-white line on this map shows its route.

routes for both military vehicles and private citizens in the event of a war with the Soviet Union. He had seen the German autobahn system during World War II and pushed Congress to pass legislation that would give the United States a similar network of highways.

Construction began in 1956—Kansas and Missouri both claim to have built the first segments. It took 37 years to finish the project, which was later named the Dwight D. Eisenhower System of Interstate and Defense Highways. The last link in the 42,800-mile (68,865-km) system was completed in Los Angeles, California, in 1993.

Hawaii has three interstate highways—not to connect it to other states, but to provide good roads to the state's three key military areas. Alaska is the only state without an interstate highway.

What do the numbers of interstate highways mean?

You can tell whether an interstate highway runs north–south or east–west by its one- or two-digit number. Odd-numbered interstates run north–south, and the numbers increase as you travel from the West Coast (I-5) to the East coast (I-95). Even-numbered interstates run east–west, and the numbers increase as you go from south (I-10) to north (I-94). In some cases an interstate doesn't run exactly north to south or east to west, so a number was assigned based on the road's general direction.

Interstate highways with three digits are those that connect to other major highways. If the first number is an

Safety on Interstate Highways

Statistically speaking, it is safer to drive on interstate highways than on other kinds of roads in the United States. The fatality rate on interstates is 50 percent lower, and the injury rate is 70 percent lower. Interstates were designed with safety in mind: there are no intersections and no railroad crossings, curves are engineered for safety at high speeds, lanes are divided in each direction, and grades are moderated to eliminate blind hills.

even number, it means the highway connects to another interstate highway at both ends—such as a beltway or a loop around a city. If the first digit is an odd number, the highway is usually a spur route, which means it connects with an interstate at one end only—for example, a road that goes into a city.

What are those green or white signs with numbers that are placed along interstate highways?

They're mile markers, and they give travelers a way to determine where they are along a route. The mile marker shows the number of miles from where the interstate route entered the state you are in. For north–south highways, the numbering begins at the state line in the south; for east–west highways, it begins with the state line in the west. If the interstate originates within a state, the counting starts where the highway begins.

What was the first highway in the United States?

The first federal highway had several names: the National Road, the Cumberland Road, and the National Pike. It was begun in 1811 in Cumberland, Maryland, and by 1841 it ran almost 800 miles, to Vandalia, Illinois. This road was important because it provided a route over the Allegheny Mountains and linked the Potomac and Ohio Rivers. It was quite a road for its day, at 20 feet (6 m) wide and covered with 18 inches (46 cm) of crushed stone. Today, U.S. Route 40 (not to be confused with Interstate 40) closely follows the original road.

Does the Cumberland Road pass through the Cumberland Gap?

No, not even close. The Cumberland Gap is near the place where Kentucky, Virginia, and Tennessee meet. It's a natural cut in the Cumberland Mountains that was formed millions of years ago by water cutting through the Cumberland Plateau. In 1775, Daniel Boone blazed the Wilderness Trail, which runs through the Cumberland Gap. He was employed by a group of people who hoped to make Kentucky the fourteenth U.S. state. This trail became a primary route for American settlers moving west.

What's the busiest airport in the United States?

Atlanta, Georgia, has the busiest airport in the United States, no matter how you measure it: either by number of passengers getting on or off a plane (passengers who are just passing through don't count) or by the number of takeoffs and landings. Chicago's O'Hare International Airport comes in second, followed by the Los Angeles and Dallas–Fort Worth airports.

Those four U.S. airports are also the world's busiest airports. By number of passengers, they are followed by London (Heathrow), Tokyo, Frankfurt, and Paris (Charles de Gaulle).

What are the biggest U.S. farm states?

California leads the country in agricultural production, followed in order by Texas, Iowa, Kansas, and Nebraska.

North Dakota produces the most wheat, followed by Kansas. Iowa produces the most corn, followed by Illinois and Nebraska. Texas produces the most cotton, followed by California and Mississippi.

Texas produces the most cattle, followed by Kansas and Nebraska. Iowa leads the states in hog production, followed by North Carolina. Arkansas is tops in poultry production.

Are there any fish farms in the United States?

Yes—in fact, every state in the nation has at least a few fish farms. Salmon is raised in the waters off Maine and Alaska. Arkansas and Mississippi, in particular, have many large catfish farms. Idaho's trout farms produce 80 percent of the world's farm-raised trout. Louisiana, Texas, Maryland, and Virginia are also big fish and shellfish farming states. The practice of raising fish in ponds and tanks as well as pens and cages in offshore areas is called aquaculture.

Is gold still mined in the United States?

Yes; in fact, the United States is a major source of gold—second in the world after South Africa. Most gold comes from mines in Alaska and a few other western states. Most U.S. gold comes from just 25 mines.

The United States is also in second place worldwide for copper production, after Chile.

Which states produce the most energy resources?

Wyoming, West Virginia, and Kentucky produce most of the nation's coal. Natural gas comes mainly from Texas, New Mexico, Wyoming, and Oklahoma as well as from federal offshore sites in the Gulf of Mexico. There are huge reserves of natural gas in Arkansas and Oklahoma. More than half of U.S. electricity is generated using coal, and almost a fourth of U.S. homes are heated with natural gas.

Is wind being used to generate electricity in the United States today?

Yes, mostly in the western part of the country. The federal government has set a goal to use wind power to produce at least 5 percent of the nation's electricity by 2020. Large-scale wind farms are operating in California, Texas, Minnesota, Iowa, Wisconsin, Colorado, and Oregon, and several other states are experimenting with this nonpolluting method of energy production. In all, about 13,000 windmills were generating electricity in the United States in 2000.

One of the largest wind farms is near Storm Lake, in northwestern Iowa. It uses 257 wind turbines—tall towers with propellerlike blades at the top—to convert the kinetic power of the wind into mechanical power, which generators then convert into electricity. This electricity is then transferred to a local utility grid for use by customers.

The world's largest wind generation plant, with 470 windmills, is on the Washington-Oregon border, overlooking the Columbia River.

How big are these wind turbines?

They come in many shapes and sizes. The largest turbine, in Hawaii, is 20 stories high and has propellers with a span longer than a football field. It can produce enough electricity to power 1,400 homes. Smaller machines have blades between 8 and 25 feet (2.4 and 7.6 m) in diameter mounted on towers up to 30 feet (9 m) high.

Where are the best places in the United States for producing wind energy?

Places that have an average annual wind speed of at least 13 miles (21 km) per hour are best. These can be found along the East Coast, the Appalachian Mountains, the Great Plains, the Pacific Northwest, and a few other locations.

North Dakota is a prime location for wind power—that state has enough wind to supply 36 percent of the electricity used in the 48 conterminous states. But getting all that electricity from North Dakota to other states is the difficult part.

Is much power in the United States generated from geothermal sources?

No; less than two-tenths of 1 percent of our electricity comes from harnessing power from natural steam sources below the Earth's surface.

Who uses the most water in the United States?

Most of the nation's water is put to industrial uses, including power generation. Almost as much, about 40 percent, is used for irrigation, particularly in states like California, Texas, and Nebraska. Only 12 percent is used by households and businesses.

Which states use the most water?

California leads the list, using almost 11 percent of the nation's freshwater. Most of this water is used to irrigate crops. Next are Texas, Illinois, and Idaho, which together use about 28 percent.

How much water does the average U.S. household use each day?

Each person uses from 80 to 200 gallons (303 to 757 l) of water a day. Most of that is used to flush toilets.

PART II

THE STATES

NEW ENGLAND

Which states make up the region called New England? • Why are people from New England called Yankees? • Where is the easternmost point in the United States? • Why wasn't Maine one of the original American colonies? • What is the highest mountain in New England? • Why do some people who work in Massachusetts like to live across the border in New Hampshire? • Why is New Hampshire called the Granite State? • Do all six New England states lie along the Atlantic coastline? • Which state was the first to enter the Union after the original 13 states? • Isn't there a lake in Massachusetts with a very long Indian name? • How did Cape Cod get its name? •

State and Capital	Name Origin	Nickname	State Bird	State Flower	Land Area in Square Miles (sq km)	2000 Population
Maine (Augusta)	From "Mainland," used by explorers to distinguish from offshore islands	Pine Tree State	Chickadee	White pine cone and tassel	30,933 (80,426)	1,274,923
New Hampshire (Concord)	For a county in England	Granite State	Purple finch	Purple lilac	9,279 (24,125)	1,235,786
Vermont (Montpelier)	From French words *vert mont* (green mountain)	Green Mountain State	Hermit thrush	Red clover	9,609 (24,983)	608,827
Massachu- setts (Boston)	From Indian name for Great Blue Hill south of Boston, meaning—"place of great hill"	Bay State	Chickadee	Mayflower	7,824 (20,342)	6,349,097
Rhode Island and Providence Plantations (Providence)	For one of its 36 islands and the mainland	Ocean State	Rhode Island red	Violet	1,212 (3,151)	1,048,319
Connecticut (Hartford)	From Indian word meaning "along the long tidal river"	Constitution State	Robin	Mountain laurel	5,018 (13,047)	3,405,565

New England

NEW
HAMPSHIRE

VERMONT

Montpelier

MAINE

Augusta

Concord

Boston

MASSACHUSETTS

Hartford

Providence

RHODE
ISLAND

CONNECTICUT

0   200 mi
0   200 km

The New England
states including
capital cities. All
have coastlines on
the Atlantic Ocean
except landlocked
Vermont.

Which states make up the region called New England?

New England consists of six states: Connecticut, Maine, Massachusetts, New Hampshire, Rhode Island, and Vermont. Captain John Smith named the region New England while exploring the northeastern coast in 1614.

In 1686 the English government formed a province they also called New England that consisted of the colonies of New Hampshire, Massachusetts (which then included Maine), Rhode Island, and Connecticut. New York and New Jersey were added 2 years later. But in 1689, the people of New England overthrew the English lord who ruled the province, and the colonies became separate again.

Why are people from New England called Yankees?

No one knows for sure. Some think "Yankee" may have been derived from *Janke,* the Dutch nickname for *Jan,* meaning "John" in English. *Janke* was considered to be an insulting name during the 1600s. By the mid-1700s, the British were using the word to refer to New Englanders in a negative way. Once the American Revolution began, New Englanders proudly adopted the nickname to refer to themselves.

Where is the easternmost point in the United States?

A small peninsula near the town of Lubec, Maine, called West Quoddy Head, lies the farthest east of the conterminous 48 U.S. states. But the U.S. Virgin Islands, a U.S. territory in the Caribbean Sea, lies a bit farther east than West Quoddy Head.

Why wasn't Maine one of the original American colonies?

Maine was a part of Massachusetts for almost 200 years. In 1820 it broke away and became the twenty-third state. For much of its early history, in the 1600s and 1700s, Maine was claimed by both the French and the British; the British finally took it at the end of the French and Indian War in 1763.

What is the highest mountain in New England?

Mount Washington, in New Hampshire, is the highest peak in New England, at 6,288 feet (1,917 m). It is part of the Presidential Range, which has mountains named for Presidents Adams, Jefferson, Monroe, and Madison.

New Hampshire's mountain areas include five monadnocks, which are mountains or hills that sit alone on a flat plain because the rock they are made of has resisted erosion. They are Mount Moosilauke (the tallest, at 4,810 feet/[1,466 m]), Mount Monadnock, Mount Cardigan, Mount Kearsarge, and Sunapee Mountain.

Maine is the leading producer of toothpicks in the United States. It's called the Pine Tree State, but its toothpicks are made of white birch, not pine. The state is also the third leading U.S. producer of potatoes.

Why do some people who work in Massachusetts like to live across the border in New Hampshire?

Because New Hampshire does not have a general sales tax or a state income tax on individual earned income. The state does levy other kinds of taxes, but even so, it has the third lowest overall taxes of all the states.

New Hampshire has just 13 miles (21 km) of coastline on the Atlantic Ocean—the shortest coastline of any state that borders an ocean.

Why is New Hampshire called the Granite State?

New Hampshire, like several other New England states, contains large deposits of granite, a very hard and durable igneous rock used as building material. It was once a major supplier of granite to other states, and several granite quarries continue to operate there.

Do all six New England states lie along the Atlantic coastline?

All but Vermont. However, Vermont's west and east borders are mainly water—Lake Champlain forms a good part of its western border with New York, and the Connecticut River forms Vermont's entire eastern border with New Hampshire.

Vermont is the most rural of all the states. Two-thirds of its residents live outside cities.

Which state was the first to enter the Union after the original 13 states?

Vermont. It was an independent republic until 1791, when it joined the Union. The original 13 states were New Hampshire, Massachusetts, Connecticut, Rhode Island, New York, New Jersey, Pennsylvania, Delaware, Maryland, Virginia, North Carolina, South Carolina, and Georgia.

About half the cranberries grown in the United States come from southeastern Massachusetts, Cape Cod, and nearby islands.

Isn't there a lake in Massachusetts with a very long Indian name?

Yes. The Indian name for Lake Webster is Lake Chaubunagungamaug. And that's the short form. The long form is Chargoggagoggmanchauggagoggchaubunagungamaug. Translated, it means "You fish your side of the lake. I fish my side. Nobody fishes the middle."

The Original 13 Colonies

NEW HAMPSHIRE
NEW YORK
PENNSYLVANIA
MASSACHUSETTS
RHODE ISLAND
CONNECTICUT
NEW JERSEY
DELAWARE
MARYLAND
VIRGINIA
NORTH CAROLINA
SOUTH CAROLINA
GEORGIA

0   400 miles
0   400 km

How did Cape Cod get its name?

Cape Cod is a 65-mile (105-km)-long peninsula of Massachusetts that is a popular East Coast summer vacation area. It's easy to find on maps because of the distinctive hook at its far end. It was originally named Pallavisino by the first European to spot it, the Italian explorer Giovanni da Verrazano, in 1524.

In 1602, the English explorer Bartholomew Gosnold stumbled on it while searching for a shortcut to Asia. He renamed it Cape Cod because of the abundance of huge cod fish in its waters. Cod became extremely important to the New England economy for several hundred years. In recent decades, though, overfishing has greatly reduced the number of cod in the Atlantic.

The original 13 colonies did not include Vermont, which was at different times claimed by New York and by New Hampshire and existed as an independent republic of Maine, which was part of Massachusetts.

Beaches facing protected Cape Cod Bay have calm waters offshore; fierce ocean waves pound the shores facing the Atlantic.

Massachusetts has a state fish: the cod. A sculpture of a cod fish hangs in the Massachusetts House of Representatives to remind people of the importance of cod to the state's economy in the past.

Massachusetts is notable for three sports firsts. Basketball was invented in Springfield in 1891 by James Naismith, who wanted to devise a game that could be played indoors in the winter. Volleyball was developed by the director of the Holyoke, Massachusetts, YMCA in 1895. And the very first baseball World Series game was played in Boston on October 1, 1903.

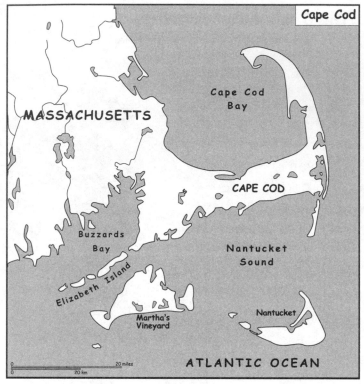

Why is Massachusetts called a commonwealth?

Massachusetts and three other states—Kentucky, Pennsylvania, and Virginia—are called commonwealths, but they are also states of the United States. There is no legal difference between the terms "commonwealth" and "state," and they are used interchangeably. The only *true* U.S. commonwealth, meaning a self-governing, autonomous political unit voluntarily associated with the United States, is Puerto Rico. (For more on Puerto Rico, see page 49.)

How did Rhode Island get its name? The state isn't really an island.

The smallest U.S. state has the longest official name: "Rhode Island and Providence Plantations." Providence Plantations refers to the towns on the mainland. The island of Rhode Island—now more commonly called Aquidneck —is the largest of thirty-six islands (most of which are in Narragansett Bay) that also make up the state.

Rhode Island, First and Last

Rhode Island was the first of the 13 American colonies to declare its independence from Great Britain. It did so on May 4, 1776, exactly 2 months to the day before the other 12 colonies. Rhode Island was the only one of the 13 colonies that did not attend the Constitutional Convention in Philadelphia in 1787, and it was the last state to ratify the Constitution, in 1790. Its representatives did not want to approve the Constitution until it included the Bill of Rights, which guaranteed individual liberties and limited the powers of the federal government.

The city of Newport and two smaller towns are on the 44-square-mile (114-sq-km) island of Aquidneck. The land area of the state of Rhode Island is 1,045 square miles (2,717 sq km), which is half the size of Delaware, the next smallest state. With more than 400 miles (644 km) of shoreline, Rhode Island is known as the Ocean State.

Small as it is, Rhode Island is still larger than six of the world's countries, both in land area and population. Those countries—all in Europe—are Andorra, Liechtenstein, Malta, Monaco, San Marino, and Vatican City.

Does Rhode Island have the smallest population of all the states?

No; Rhode Island ranks 43rd among the 50 states in population, with a little more than 1 million people. States with fewer people (in order after Rhode Island) are Montana, South Dakota, Delaware, North Dakota, Alaska, Vermont, and Wyoming.

Why is Connecticut nicknamed the Constitution State?

In 1639, the colony of Connecticut established its Fundamental Orders, which set up a government based on the will of the people. Some historians say that this document was the first ever written constitution of a democratic government and may have served as a model for the U.S. Constitution. Also, during the writing of the U.S. Constitution in 1787, the delegates from Connecticut helped resolve an argument over how many representatives each state could send to Congress. Their solution was referred to as the Connecticut Compromise, and it may be another reason why Connecticut is called the Constitution State.

The Hartford (Conn.) Courant began publishing in 1764, making it the longest continuously published newspaper in the United States today.

Although most of Connecticut's farm income comes from eggs and dairy products, an expensive type of tobacco is grown in the central part of the state and is used to make cigar wrappings.

What do you call a person from Connecticut?

A "Connecticuter," says *Webster's New International Dictionary,* although there is no official state term to describe a person who was born in or lives in Connecticut. In the 1700s two other words were seen in print: "Connecticotian" and "Connecticutensian." At one time, "Nutmegger" was used to refer to a person from Connecticut because of another state nickname, the Nutmeg State. In the state's early days, Connecticut peddlers traveled around New England selling nutmegs.

Connecticut: The Insurance State

Connecticut is often called the Insurance State because it is headquarters for more than 100 insurance companies. In the 1790s companies there began insuring ships and cargo that left its ports. These companies prospered, and by 1810 people could buy insurance that would cover them for "loss of life or personal injury while journeying by railway or steamboat."

CHAPTER 6

THE MID-ATLANTIC

s the Empire State Building in New York City the tallest building in the United States? ◆ Is it true that New York City was once the capital of the United States? ◆ Why is New York called the Empire State? ◆ Why is New York City called the Big Apple? ◆ Why do Buffalo and other cities in upstate New York always seem to get so much snow? ◆ Why was New York City once called New Amsterdam? ◆ What are the names of New York City's five boroughs? ◆ Why was the Erie Canal such a significant achievement? ◆ What are the Finger Lakes in New York State? ◆ Why is Pennsylvania called the Keystone State? ◆ Who are the Pennsylvania Dutch people? ◆ Is it true that the Amish

State and Capital	Name Origin	Nickname	State Bird	State Flower	Land Area in Square Miles (sq km)	2000 Population
New York (Albany)	For the duke of York	Empire State	Bluebird	Rose	49,576 (128,898)	18,976,457
Pennsylvania (Harrisburg)	For the father of William Penn, founder of the colony	Keystone State	Ruffed grouse	Mountain laurel	45,333 (117,865)	12,281,054
New Jersey (Trenton)	For the Isle of Jersey in England	Garden State	Eastern goldfinch	Purple violet	7,787 (20,246)	8,414,350
Delaware (Dover)	For Lord De La Warr	First State	Blue hen chicken	Peach blossom	2,057 (5,348)	783,600
Maryland (Annapolis)	For Queen Henrietta Maria of England	Old Line State	Baltimore oriole	Black-eyed Susan	10,460 (27,196)	5,296,486

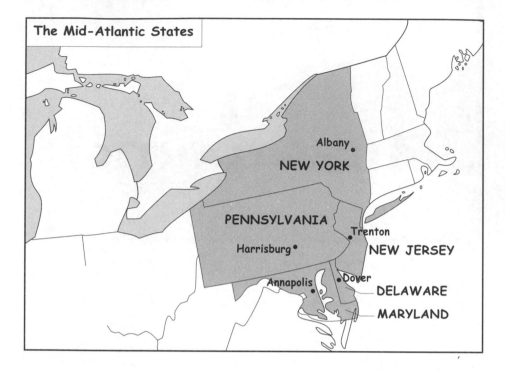

The Mid-Atlantic States

The Mid-Atlantic states including capital cities. These states have traditionally been centers of business and government. Their importance as manufacturing states has declined.

Is the Empire State Building in New York City the tallest building in the United States?

No. The Sears Tower, in Chicago, Illinois, is the tallest, at 1,450 feet (442 m), with 110 floors. The Empire State Building is the second tallest building in the country. It rises 1,250 feet (381 m) and has 102 stories. The Empire State Building was built in 1931 and was the world's tallest building for many years.

Is it true that New York City was once the capital of the United States?

Yes, New York was the capital between 1785 and 1790. George Washington was sworn in as the first president there in 1789. In 1790 Congress agreed, as part of a compromise between northern and southern leaders, to locate a permanent capital along the banks of the Potomac River. In the meantime, the temporary capital was moved to Philadelphia in 1790, part of another political compromise.

Within its official city limits, New York City has a population of 7.4 million—more people than live in 39 of the 50 states.

Why is New York called the Empire State?

It's not because of the Empire State Building—the state had its nickname long before 1931, when that famous skyscraper was built. No one knows for sure, but some historians think the name can be traced to George Washington, who once said the state might become the seat of a new empire.

Why is New York City called the Big Apple?

The latest theory is that horse-racing trainers and jockeys in the 1920s used the term to refer to New York City, where racetracks offered winners large purses—in other words, a big treat, or a "big apple."

Why are there skyscrapers in two distinct areas of Manhattan—lower Manhattan and midtown—but few very tall buildings between those two areas?

The answer has to do with the geology of Manhattan Island. Very tall buildings need a very solid foundation, and Manhattan Island's bedrock of schist (a granitelike rock) is particularly solid and stable. In lower Manhattan the schist is about 80 feet (24 m) below street level, and in midtown it lies about 38 feet (12 m) below street level. But in between the two areas, the schist is more than 200 feet (61 m) deep—way too far for skyscraper builders to dig to reach bedrock.

Why do Buffalo and other cities in upstate New York always seem to get so much snow?

Buffalo, Syracuse, and Rochester do receive much more snow than most U.S. cities—only Juneau, Alaska, and Sault Ste. Marie, Michigan, have averaged more snow than Buffalo over the past half century. The reason is upstate New York's proximity to the Great Lakes, whose huge expanses of open water provide ample moisture for snow and rain to develop in the area. Cold arctic air blows over the lakes, bringing precipitation to the area. This phenomenon is referred to as lake-effect snow. Buffalo's annual average snowfall is 92 inches (234 cm). New York City, in contrast, gets about 28 inches (71 cm) of snow annually.

In the first few decades of the nation's history, Virginia was the most populous state. But by 1810 New York had taken over. It remained number one for more than 150 years, until California passed it in population in the 1960s. By the 1990s, Texas also had more people than New York.

Why was New York City once called New Amsterdam?

Henry Hudson, an Englishman, was hired by the Dutch to find a shortcut to the Pacific Ocean back in the early 1600s. When he sailed up the river now named for him, he was able to claim the land around it—today's states of New York, New Jersey, Delaware, and part of Connecticut—for the Netherlands. This area was called New Netherland, and the town the Dutch settled in 1625 on Manhattan Island was called New Amsterdam, named after the city in the Netherlands. Some Dutch names remain in the New York City area today. For example, the borough of Brooklyn was originally the Dutch town of Breuckelen.

The English and the Dutch fought for many years in the mid-1600s for control of this region. When the English finally won control of the colony in a peace treaty in 1674, it was renamed New York, after the duke of York. The duke's brother, King Charles II of England, had given him a charter for the land.

What are the names of New York City's five boroughs?

The city's five boroughs are also counties: Bronx (Bronx County), Brooklyn (Kings County), Manhattan (New York County), Queens (Queens County), and Staten Island (Richmond County).

Queens is the largest in area, with 108 square miles (281 sq km), while Brooklyn (Kings County) is the largest in population, with 2.3 million people.

Why was the Erie Canal such a significant achievement?

Once the Erie Canal was completed in 1825, it connected New York City (via the Hudson River) with Buffalo, New York, which is on Lake Erie. From there, barges and boats could reach areas of the upper Midwest by way of the Great Lakes. In those days, roads were hardly more than rough trails, and traveling west over the Allegheny Mountains was difficult, slow, and expensive. This new transportation route made trade

The Erie Canal Today

In the years after the Erie Canal opened in 1825, the canals were enlarged twice and finally mostly abandoned in the early 1900s, when the New York State Barge Canal was opened to accommodate the larger barges of the day. This new waterway was created by dredging out and damming the rivers the Erie Canal had bypassed.

When the St. Lawrence Seaway opened in 1959, shippers on the Great Lakes had a better way to get to sea, and New York's canal system began to lose business. Today the canal system is used for recreational activities. Only pleasure boats use the canals, and many of the old towpaths have been turned into biking and hiking trails.

between East Coast businesses and Midwest farmers much easier, cheaper, and faster. As a result, the economy grew and more people prospered. The Erie Canal helped New York City grow to become a world commercial center, and it also spurred settlement of the American West.

The Erie Canal was an engineering marvel. In just 8 years, men working only with the help of horses dug a waterway that was 363 miles (584 km) long, 40 feet (12 m) wide, and 4 feet (1.2 m) deep. They also had to build 83 locks so that barges could cross the 500-foot (152 m) rise in elevation west of Troy, New York.

What are the Finger Lakes in New York State?

The Finger Lakes, in west-central New York, got their name because their long, narrow shapes look like fingers of a hand. There are 11 lakes in the group, although some people disagree on that number. The largest is Lake Seneca, at 37 miles (60 km) long and 3 miles (5 km) wide (at its widest point).

These lakes were formed when glaciers—which covered the state with ice that was up to 2 miles (3.2 km) thick—cut deep valleys in the area. When those glaciers began to melt and recede about 10,000 years ago, water filled the valleys. Glacial deposits of sand and rock kept

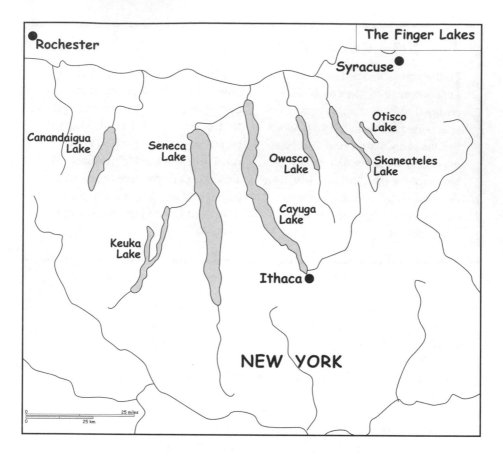

The long, deep Finger Lakes were cut by glaciers. Their names come from Native American words.

William Penn, founder of Pennsylvania, named his colony in honor of his father, Admiral Sir William Penn of England.

the water from draining out of the ends of the valleys, and the lakes were created.

Why is Pennsylvania called the Keystone State?

In architecture, the keystone is the wedge-shaped stone that is placed in an arch to hold the other stones in place. In 1802, at a state rally celebrating the presidential victory of Thomas Jefferson, someone made a toast to Pennsylvania that called it "the keystone in the federal union," a reference to the state's key role in the development of the new nation.

Another nickname for Pennsylvania is the Quaker State, which comes from the fact that the founder of the Pennsylvania colony, William Penn, and many of the settlers who joined him were Quakers. Penn established his colony on the principles of religious tolerance.

Who are the Pennsylvania Dutch people?

The people called Pennsylvania Dutch are not Dutch at all, but rather descendants of the many German immigrants who settled in the central part of the state beginning in the 1700s. The German word for German is *Deutsch,* which was mispronounced as "Dutch."

Today, many Pennsylvania Dutch people still live in the central part of the state, especially around Lancaster. Some—but not all—of them are members of a religious group called Old Order Amish.

Is it true that the Amish people in Pennsylvania don't believe in driving cars or using electricity?

About 18,000 of the nation's Old Order Amish (pronounced *Ah*-mish) people live in and around Lancaster, Pennsylvania. The Amish religion is an offshoot of the Mennonite faith. People of both these denominations came to America in the early 1700s, with many settling in Pennsylvania, to escape religious persecution in Europe.

The Amish emphasize the importance of humility, family, community, and separation from the world. For that reason they do not use electricity because they wish to keep their lives both simple and isolated from outside influences, which electrical devices such as radio and television could bring into their homes. Many use horses and buggies rather than cars to get around. Old Order Amish keep their children home from school after they finish the eighth grade, putting them to work on the family farm or in the family business.

Why is New Jersey called the Garden State?

In the nineteenth and early twentieth centuries, New Jersey farmers played a large role in providing food to the people of nearby New York City, which may be the reason for the state's nickname. Today, although nearly 9 out of 10 people in New Jersey live in cities (only California has a higher percentage of city dwellers), the state still has many truck farms, orchards, and greenhouses. New Jersey's main crops today are tomatoes, sweet corn, peaches, blueberries, and cranberries.

The world's largest chocolate and candy factory is in Hershey, Pennsylvania.

Pennsylvania is the nation's top mushroom-producing state. It accounts for more than 40 percent of all U.S. production, which totaled 800 million pounds (360 million kg) in 1998. Mushrooms are grown in cool, dark houses specially constructed for the purpose.

New Jersey is the nation's most densely populated state, with 1,094 people per square mile. It ranks ninth in population among the 50 states.

Why is Delaware called the First State?

Delaware was the first state to ratify the U.S. Constitution, which it did on December 7, 1787. That's why Delaware is represented first in presidential inaugurations and other national events.

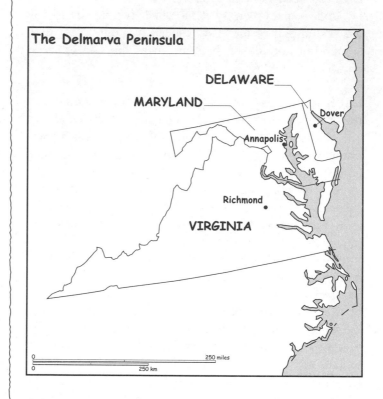

The Delmarva Peninsula

Delaware, Maryland, and Virginia share the Delmarva Peninsula.

Delaware Combinations

A few interesting geographic names have come from combining Delaware's name with those of its neighbors. The strip of land that extends between the Chesapeake Bay and the Atlantic Ocean contains all of Delaware and parts of Maryland and Virginia. The popular name for the entire area is the Delmarva Peninsula—formed from *DEL*aware, *MAR*yland, and Virgini*A*. The names of two Delaware/Maryland border towns—Delmar and Marydel—also are formed using letters from the two state names.

Who were the first Europeans to settle in Delaware?

People from Sweden and Finland settled near present-day Wilmington in 1638, calling their colony New Sweden. These settlers built log cabins much like those they had in Scandinavia. Later that century, the Dutch and then the English took over the colony. Since local forests offered a plentiful supply of logs for building, the log cabin style of housing was quickly adopted by American settlers from other lands.

For whom was the state of Maryland named?

The state was named for Queen Henrietta Maria, who was the wife of King Charles I of England. In 1632 King Charles granted the land that was to become Maryland to Cecilius Calvert, and he and his descendants ran the colony for many years. Calvert, a Roman Catholic, wanted to establish a colony where Catholics from England could worship without persecution.

Does the Chesapeake Bay contain freshwater or salt water?

The Chesapeake Bay—bordered by Maryland and Virginia—is the nation's largest estuary. An estuary is an arm of a sea that extends inland to meet the mouth of a river. The Chesapeake Bay contains mostly salt water, since it is part of the Atlantic Ocean. But freshwater from many rivers and streams flow into the bay and dilute the salt water. Many kinds of fish and shellfish live in its waters, and the surrounding area attracts a variety of migratory birds. All told, about 2,700 species of plants and animals live in the region.

Maryland is known for its abundant seafood—the Chesapeake Bay provides half of the nation's blue crab harvest each year. Other seafood products from Maryland include clams, oysters, striped bass, flounder, spot, croaker, sea trout, and bluefish.

Where does the name "Chesapeake" come from?

The Native Americans who once lived along the bay gave it an Algonquian name, Chesepiook, meaning "great shellfish bay."

If you look at a map, you'll notice that Delaware's northern boundary with Pennsylvania is formed by the arc of a perfect circle. It's the only state with a circular boundary.

PENNSYLVANIA

Chesapeake Bay Area

Dover

Baltimore

DELAWARE

Annapolis

Washington

DISTRICT OF COLUMBIA

MARYLAND

Salisbury

CHESAPEAKE BAY

EASTERN SHORE

VIRGINIA

Norfolk

Virginia Beach

0   100 miles
0   100 km

Is Baltimore still an important port city?

Its central location has kept Baltimore, Maryland, an active port city on the Chesapeake Bay for more than 300 years. Baltimore is closer to the American Midwest than any other East Coast port, and it is just an overnight drive for a third of the U.S. population.

Raising Fish on Farms

Traditional fishing is being supplemented by the practice of aquaculture in Maryland, in which growers use ponds or special tanks to raise millions of pounds of trout, striped bass, catfish, and tilapia, and lesser amounts of oysters and soft crabs each year. Overfishing and pollution have resulted in smaller fish and shellfish catches in the Chesapeake Bay over the past several decades.

Oceangoing ships can reach the port of Baltimore from the Atlantic Ocean in two ways: through the Chesapeake and Delaware Canal in Cecil County, or through the mouth of the Chesapeake Bay between the Virginia capes.

THE MIDWEST

State and Capital	Name Origin	Nickname	State Bird	State Flower	Land Area in Square Miles (sq km)	2000 Population
Ohio (Columbus)	For the Ohio River; Iroquois Indian word for "something great"	Buckeye State	Cardinal	Scarlet carnation	41,222 (107,177)	11,353,140
Indiana (Indianapolis)	Means "Land of the Indians"	Hoosier State	Cardinal	Peony	36,291 (94,357)	6,080,485
Illinois (Springfield)	From Illini Indian word *illiniwek*, meaning "superior men"	Land of Lincoln	Cardinal	Native violet	56,400 (146,640)	12,419,293
Michigan (Lansing)	For Lake Michigan, after *michigama*, Chippewa Indian word for "great or large lake"	Wolverine State	Robin	Apple blossom	58,216 (218,577)	9,938,444
Wisconsin (Madison)	From Indian word possibly meaning "homeland," "wild rice country," or "gathering of the waters"	Badger State	Robin	Wood violet	56,154 (146,000)	5,363,675
Minnesota (St. Paul)	From Sioux Indian words meaning "sky-tinted waters"	Gopher State	Common loon	Pink and white lady's slipper	84,068 (218,577)	4,919,479
Iowa (Des Moines)	From Indian Word meaning "beautiful land" or "one who puts to sleep"	Hawkeye State	Eastern goldfinch	Wild rose	56,290 (146,354)	2,926,324

State and Capital	Name Origin	Nickname	State Bird	State Flower	Land Area in Square Miles (sq km)	2000 Population
Missouri (Jefferson City)	After the Missouri River, from an Indian word meaning "town of the large canoes"	Show Me State	Bluebird	Hawthorn	69,686 (181,184)	5,595,211
North Dakota (Bismarck)	After Sioux Indian name for themselves, Dakota or Lakota, meaning "friends"	Flickertail State	Western meadow-lark	Wild prairie rose	70,665 (183,729)	642,200
South Dakota (Pierre)	Same as for North Dakota	Mount Rushmore State	Ring-necked pheasant	American pasque-flower	77,047 (200,322)	754,844
Nebraska (Lincoln)	After the Oto Indian word *nebrathka* for the Platte River, meaning "flat water"	Cornhusker State	Western meadow-lark	Goldenrod	77,227 (200,790)	1,711,263
Kansas (Topeka)	After the Kansa or Kaw Indians, meaning "people of the south wind"	Sunflower State	Western meadow-lark	Sunflower	82,264 (213,886)	2,688,418

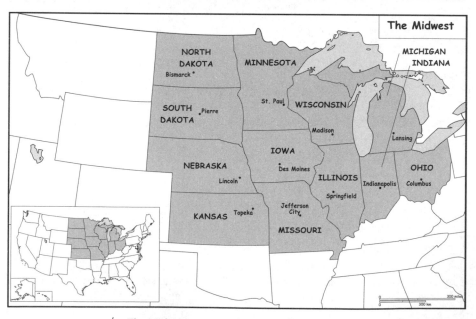

The Midwest states including capital cities. This region contains some of the most fertile farmland in the United States, as well as numerous factories and even mines.

How many U.S. presidents were born in Ohio?

Seven, more than any other state except Virginia. They were Ulysses S. Grant, Rutherford B. Hayes, James A. Garfield, Benjamin Harrison, William McKinley, William Howard Taft, and Warren G. Harding. Although he was born in Indiana, William Henry Harrison was living in Ohio when he became president.

Ohio's nickname, "The Buckeye State," comes from the buckeye tree, which was once quite common there.

Why did Ohio become such an important manufacturing state?

Geographic advantages made Ohio an ideal place for making various products. First, it has important minerals used in manufacturing, especially coal. It also has ample supplies of water. Second, products could be easily transported to other parts of the country via Lake Erie and the Erie Canal as well as by other canals, railroads, and roads. For this reason it was once known as the Gateway State. Today it remains one of the major manufacturing states, especially for automobiles and automobile parts, machinery, food products, and steel.

Who were the Mound Builders who once lived in the Ohio River Valley?

The prehistoric Indians archaeologists call the Mound Builders lived (from 800 B.C. to A.D. 500) in the area that is now the Mississippi and Ohio River Valley areas of the United States. These people built some 6,000 burial mounds, forts, and other earthen structures, some of which survive today.

One of the most impressive is an effigy mound called Serpent Mound, near Peebles, Ohio, in Adams County near the Kentucky border. This mound, which looks like an uncoiling snake, averages 3 feet (91 cm) high and is almost 1,320 feet (402 m) long. Constructed about 2,000 years ago, it was evidently not a burial mound because no burial objects have ever been found in it.

Ohio has the only nonrectangular state flag. Its flag is shaped like a pennant.

Why are people from Indiana called Hoosiers?

No one knows for sure—the term has been in use since at least the 1830s—but there are lots of amusing theories. For example, early pioneers in the state supposedly

Indiana is the smallest state in land area of any state west of the Appalachian Mountains except Hawaii. Indiana is thirty-eighth in size of all the states, but it ranks fourteenth in population.

Indiana leads the nation in steel production. It is also a leading producer of aluminum and pharmaceuticals.

The Chicago River, which now flows out of Lake Michigan, used to run in the opposite direction. In 1900, engineers reversed its flow when they completed the Chicago Sanitary and Ship Canal. Today people call it "the river that flows backward."

answered a knock on the door by saying, "Who's yere?" Then there's the theory that the name came from rivermen who were good at beating up, or "hushing," their enemies, earning them the name of "hushers." Another says that a canal contractor named Hoosier liked hiring laborers from Indiana, who became known as "Hoosier's men," or just plain Hoosiers.

Another possibility is that "hoosier" was commonly used in the South in the 1800s to refer to people who lived in the hills. Many people from Cumberland, England, immigrated to America and settled in the mountains of the southeastern United States. In the dialect of the people living around Cumberland in those days, a "hoo" meant high or hill, and "hoozer" meant anything unusually large. When the descendants of these early settlers moved to Indiana, they may have brought the name with them.

Is there really a town named Santa Claus in Indiana?

Yes, and its post office receives half a million packages, letters, and cards for remailing with the town's postmark during the winter holiday season.

Why is Illinois so flat?

The highest point in Illinois—Charles Mound, near Apple River—rises only 1,235 feet (376 m). During the last Ice Age, glaciers spread across the region and flattened it. But those same glaciers left behind materials that became the fertile soils that have made Illinois a leading agricultural state.

Is the world's tallest building in Chicago?

Not any longer. Between 1973 and 1996, the Sears Tower was the tallest building in the world, but today it is the tallest in North America. It is 1,450 feet (442 m) high and has 110 stories. However, it does have the highest occupied floor (1,431 ft [436 m]) of any building in the world. The tallest buildings in the world as of 2001 are the Petronas Twin Towers in Kuala Lumpur, Malaysia; each building rises 1,483 feet (452 m) high and has 88 stories. Chicago was home to the world's first metal frame skyscraper, back in 1885 when the 10-story Home Insurance Building was completed.

The Tri-State Tornado of 1925

Murphysboro, Illinois, holds the sad record of being the U.S. city to have the most people killed in a tornado. In March 1925 a total of 234 people died in and around Murphysboro in the most destructive tornado ever in the United States. Known as the Tri-State Tornado of 1925, it set several other U.S. tornado records, including the longest continuous track on the ground (219 mi/353 km) and its duration (3.5 hours) This tornado formed over southeastern Missouri and proceeded to storm across southern Illinois and southwestern Indiana at speeds that sometimes exceeded 300 miles (483 km) per hour. When it was over, the tornado had killed 695 people, injured more than 2,000, and destroyed 15,000 homes in those three states.

How did Michigan get to be called "The Wolverine State"?

No one is sure. One theory is that valuable wolverine pelts were often brought to local trading posts, but some authorities say that isn't true because wolverines may have never lived in the area. Wolverines are voracious animals, and one story goes that the Indians in the area called the early American settlers—who were taking over their lands—by that name. Another story says that during a dispute over a piece of land, people in Ohio called the people in Michigan that name.

Why is Detroit called the Motor City?

Detroit-area automotive plants make more cars and trucks than anywhere else in the world. The world's first automobile factory was built in Detroit in 1900 by R. E. Olds, who had produced a steam-driven car in Lansing in 1886. Henry Ford established the Ford Motor Company in Detroit in 1903, and General Motors was founded there 5 years later. Michigan's vast resources of iron ore and other minerals, plus easy access to rail and water transportation, have made it a leading state for manufacturing since the early 1900s.

Motown, the well-known Detroit-based recording company, derived its name from Motor City.

The Keweenaw Peninsula, at the northern tip of the Upper Peninsula, is one of the few sources in the world for native, or pure, copper.

What, or where, is the UP?

"UP" refers to Michigan's Upper Peninsula, the stretch of land north of the main part of the state (called the Lower Peninsula). A peninsula is defined as land that projects into a body of water from the mainland. People who live in this remote and scenic part of the state often refer to themselves as "Yoopers."

Michigan's
Upper Peninsula

MICHIGAN

Lansing•

Michigan's Upper Peninsula borders lakes Superior, Michigan, and Huron.

Michigan's Two Parts

Michigan is the only state to be made up of two widely separated parts. The Lower and Upper Peninsulas are connected by the 5-mile-long (8-km)-long Mackinac (pronounced Mackinaw) Bridge, across the Straits of Mackinac.

Michigan is surrounded by water. It touches four of the five Great Lakes and has 3,288 miles (5,294 km) of shoreline; the only state to have more is Alaska. Michigan also has plenty of water within its borders, with more than 11,000 lakes. The Upper Peninsula boasts 150 waterfalls.

Where is the breakfast cereal capital of the world?

Battle Creek, Michigan, produces more cereal that anywhere else. Breakfast cereals were invented as a kind of health food a century ago for John Kellogg's patients in a Battle Creek hospital. The two men who commercialized the idea in the early 1900s were Kellogg's brother and a man named Post.

Why is Wisconsin called America's Dairyland?

Wisconsin, is the leading milk producer in the United States. Its 1.6 million dairy cows produce a year's supply of milk for 42 million people. Wisconsin also leads the states in butter and cheese production, supplying about a fourth of the nation's butter and a third of its cheese.

Why is Wisconsin nicknamed the Badger State?

Back in the early 1800s, lead miners in Wisconsin often lived in hillside caves they had dug, which people compared to the way badgers dig holes. These miners were called Badgers, and the name was eventually applied to all Wisconsin residents.

Why do Wisconsin and Minnesota have so many lakes?

Minnesota's license plate reads "Land of 10,000 Lakes," but it really has almost 12,000 lakes. And with more than 15,000 lakes, Wisconsin—especially the northern part—is a water lover's paradise. Lake Winnebago is the largest, covering 215 square miles (559 sq km).

Like so many other lakes in this part of the world, these lakes were formed when the mile-thick glaciers that once covered the northern part of North America carved out parts of the Earth that later became lakebeds. Glaciers are huge sheets of ice that pick up huge amounts of rock and debris as they move. It is these materials that erode the land underneath the glacier. Between 8,000 and 15,000 years ago, during the last Ice Age, glaciers created most of the Earth's lakes and many other dramatic geological features, including the Grand Teton Mountains in Wyoming.

In 1882 the first plant in the United States to produce electricity by using water power was built on the Fox River in Appleton, Wisconsin.

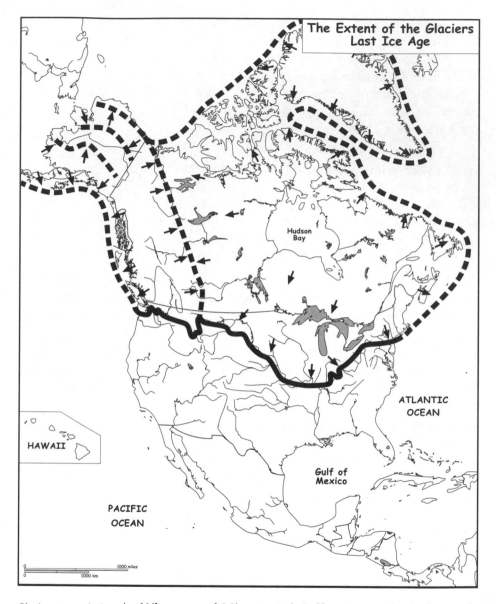

The Extent of the Glaciers Last Ice Age

Glaciers extended over much of North America during the last Ice Age. The arrows on this map show the direction of various glacier flows.

Who carved Minnesota's Jeffers petroglyphs?

Archaeologists believe that Native Americans carved pictures of people, deer, elk, turtles, spearthrowers, and other designs into areas of rock in southwestern Minnesota between 5,000 and 2,500 years ago. About 2,000 images can be seen in outcrop of red Sioux quartzite bedrock that juts out of the middle of a wide prairie.

More than 50 sites of ancient Indian rock art have been found throughout the state. There is a visitor center in Comfrey, Minnesota, where you can see and learn more about the Jeffers petroglyphs.

There is one boat for every six people in Minnesota— more than any other state.

Why is Iowa considered such an important farm state?

Iowa's soil is especially fertile and ideal for growing crops. The state has more than 100,000 farms, making it third in number of farms behind Texas and Missouri. Farmland occupies all but 8 percent of the land in Iowa; the only state with a higher percentage of farmland is Nebraska. One of 10 people in Iowa lives on a farm.

Chances are one in four that the bacon you had for breakfast came from a hog raised in Iowa; the state produces almost three times as many hogs each year as the number two hog-producing state, Illinois. Iowa grows more corn than any other state, about a fifth of all the corn in the United States. Iowa farmers often ship their grain to market via barges on the Mississippi River and less frequently on the Missouri River. Iowa is the only state to be bordered by two large navigable rivers.

What does the giant stainless steel arch in St. Louis, Missouri, symbolize?

The Gateway Arch, which sits on the Mississippi riverfront, was constructed in the early 1960s as a monument to the American pioneers who settled the western frontier. It rises 630 feet (192 m) and is the tallest man-made monument in the United States. Visitors can ride trams through the arch to a viewing area at the top,

Iowa's State Rock

Iowa has an official state rock, the geode. A geode is a round, hollow stone that, when carefully broken in half, reveals an interior of sparkling mineral crystals, usually quartz, that have grown inside. Geodes are found in great numbers in Iowa, especially in the southeastern part of the state.

The Great Flood of 1993

The most devastating flood in recent American history hit the upper and middle Mississippi Valley between late June and mid-August 1993. Flood records were broken along the Mississippi River and most of its tributaries from Minnesota to Missouri. The states worst hit were Iowa, Minnesota, Illinois, and Missouri.

A wet fall and winter had caused the ground to be saturated by the time winter snow melt and spring rains began. By June, rivers were already running at high levels throughout the region. A series of thunderstorms between June and August dumped even more water on the area. At one point in St. Louis, the Mississippi River crested at almost 50 feet (15 m)—19 feet (5.8 m) above flood stage. Altogether, more than 70,000 people in the region had to leave their homes. The floodwaters killed 52 people, destroyed nearly 50,000 homes, and damaged 12,000 square miles (31,200 sq km) of farmland.

and on a clear day they can see the horizon 30 miles (48 km) away. The Museum of Westward Expansion lies beneath the arch.

The foundations of the arch had to be sunk 60 feet (18 m) into the ground. The arch was built to withstand earthquakes, which can occur in the area (see page 45). It was designed to withstand high winds and can sway up to 18 inches (46 cm).

Did the Santa Fe Trail begin in St. Louis?

No; it started in Independence, Missouri (near Kansas City). The Santa Fe Trail was the 780-mile-long (1,256-km-long) route that settlers, cattlemen, and traders followed southwest through Kansas and either Colorado or Oklahoma to Santa Fe, New Mexico, beginning in 1821. In the early days of the trail, the area that is now the state of New Mexico was a republic of the country of Mexico.

Another important route for the western settlers was the Oregon Trail, which also began in Independence (see the questions on Oregon, page 142, for more).

Are there a lot of caves in Missouri?

Yes, Missouri has about 1,450 caves. Most lie below the Ozark Mountains in southern Missouri, where they were formed by underwater streams carving away the rock.

Which is the correct pronunciation for Missouri: Missour-ah or Missour-ee?

People in Missouri have been debating this question since the late 1800s, and people can't seem to agree. Either way is correct, according to most dictionaries.

Are there many farms in North Dakota?

Yes; farms and ranches cover 90 percent of North Dakota's land. One of every four people there works in an agriculture-related job. North Dakota is the nation's leading producer of sunflower seeds and flaxseed; it's also a major wheat producer.

What is North Dakota's most abundant natural resource?

North Dakota leads all the states in the number of coal reserves. Most of the coal is lignite, though, which does not produce as much energy as other types of coal. The state also began producing crude petroleum when reserves were discovered near Tioga in 1951.

Why are there two Dakotas—North and South?

The area of these two states was once known as the Dakota Territory, named after the tribe of Sioux Indians who lived there. Few other people settled there until the railroads began building track into the area. In the mid-1800s the U.S. government began to offer free land to settlers, who soon realized how rich the soil was. The word got out, and in the 20 years between 1870 and 1890 the population grew from 2,400 to more than 190,000 people. These early farms were so profitable they were called "bonanza farms." Many immigrants from Europe settled there during that time, especially people from Norway and Germany.

Missouri is one of two states in the nation that is bordered by eight other states. The other is Tennessee. Missouri is bordered by Iowa, Nebraska, Kansas, Oklahoma, Arkansas, Tennessee, Kentucky, and Illinois. Tennessee is bordered by Kentucky, Missouri, Arkansas, Mississippi, Alabama, Georgia, North Carolina, and Virginia.

Farmers in North Dakota produce enough wheat each year to make 108 billion sandwiches.

North Dakota has the smallest proportion of land area covered by forest of any state—less than 1 percent.

To make it easier to govern people living in widely scattered settlements, Congress split the territory into two parts. The two Dakotas became states on the same day in 1889.

Is it true that Native Americans are the largest minority in both North and South Dakota?

Yes; they represent about 4 percent in North Dakota and 7 percent in South Dakota, making them the largest minority group in each state.

How did the Black Hills of South Dakota get their name?

The Black Hills is a mountain range that lies in western South Dakota and northeastern Wyoming. These mountains are called black because they look so dark when viewed from a distance, an effect created by dense pine forests and deep valleys. The highest peak in the range, Harney Peak, is 7,242 feet (2,520 m) high.

What did General George Custer's men discover in the Black Hills?

In 1874, while on a military expedition, Custer's men found gold in the Black Hills. It didn't take long for the word to get out and attract thousands of gold hunters to the area. This led to a conflict with the resident Native American tribes—called the Black Hills War—in which the Native Americans defeated Custer and his troops at the Battle of Little Big Horn. But the Native Americans were eventually forced out, and the gold mine called the Homestake began producing more gold than any mine in the United States.

Is gold still produced in South Dakota?

Yes, and the Homestake Mine is still in operation. South Dakota continues to be one of the leading gold producers in the United States. The mine is near Deadwood, which attracted such characters as Wild Bill Hickok and Calamity Jane in the gold rush days.

Where is Mount Rushmore?

It is in the Black Hills of South Dakota. This amazing sculpture—one of the largest in the world—of the heads of George Washington, Thomas Jefferson, Theodore Roosevelt, and Abraham Lincoln was begun in 1927 and took the sculptor 14 years to complete.

Not far away, a huge sculpture is being carved of Chief Crazy Horse as a memorial to the Native American. It will be the largest sculpture in the world when it is finished, at 563 feet (172 m) high and 641 feet (195 m) long. The face of the chief's horse was completed in 1998; it is nine stories high.

What is the Ogallala aquifer?

Aquifers are like huge underground lakes—geologists define them as being a layer of water-bearing rock through which groundwater travels. The High Plains aquifer, of which the Ogallala aquifer is a part, supplies Nebraska and several other states with water for homes, farms, and industry. Almost all of Nebraska sits above this huge aquifer, which extends from South Dakota to Texas.

Nebraska has the only state legislature to have just one house, not the usual two (a house of representatives and a senate). This one-house form of government is known as unicameral.

Why have so many fossilized animal bones been discovered in Nebraska?

About 10 million years ago a volcano erupted in the Rocky Mountains more than 1,000 miles (1,610 km) to the west, sending tons of volcanic ash into the Nebraska area and burying alive hundreds of ancient animals—in particular, rhinoceros, deer, three-toed horses, and camels. Their skeletons were preserved by volcanic materials.

You can see some of their remains at Ashfall Fossil Beds State Historical Park, located in the northeastern part of the state. In the early 1970s a paleontologist discovered a fossilized rhino skull in a spot where heavy rains washed away several layers of soil at the edge of a cornfield. More than 100 rhino skeletons have been unearthed there since. One of the world's largest mammoth fossils was discovered in Wellfleet, Nebraska, in the 1920s.

What was the Dust Bowl of the 1930s?

The Dust Bowl was a region in the U.S. Great Plains—especially the states of Kansas, Colorado, New Mexico, Oklahoma, and Texas—that was hit by destructive wind and dust storms between 1934 and 1938. Millions of acres of farmland were damaged.

The situation developed because of poor farming and grazing practices, making the soil dry and loose and easily blown away by the wind. To make matters worse, a drought had been in place for several years. The first major storm struck in 1934 and carried millions of tons of dirt to places hundreds of miles east. Farmers and their families were devastated, and many moved out of the area.

What is the Great Plains?

The Great Plains is defined as the vast grassland region in central North America that extends from northern Canada into New Mexico and Texas in the United

The Great Plains stretch from Canada to Texas and take up much of Montana, the Dakotas, Nebraska, and Kansas. The part of Colorado east of the Rockies and parts of Texas, Oklahoma, New Mexico, and eastern Wyoming are covered by these flatlands as well.

States. It also covers parts of Montana, North Dakota, South Dakota, Nebraska, Colorado, Kansas, and Oklahoma. The Great Plains is one of the most important wheat-growing areas in the world. The region also has huge deposits of oil and coal.

Why was Kansas once called the Jayhawker State?

Back in the years before the Civil War in the mid-1800s, pro-Union guerrilla fighters who roamed throughout Kansas and Missouri were called Jayhawkers; they opposed those who wanted Kansas to be admitted to the Union as a slave state. No one is sure where the term comes from; some sources cite a mythical bird called the jayhawk that would torment its victims.

Kansas is the leading state in wheat production, but it is also in the top 10 for mineral production, in particular salt. It's also the leading producer of helium in the United States.

Immigrants from Russia who settled in Kansas in the 1870s unknowingly helped make Kansas the leading wheat-producing state. They had brought seeds of Turkey Red Winter wheat with them, and luckily it was the perfect variety of wheat for the Kansas climate.

s the District of Columbia a state? ◆ What else is or
Capitol Hill besides the U.S. Capitol? ◆ Why is Virginia
called the Mother of States? ◆ Why is Virginia also known
as the Mother of Presidents? ◆ What's so unusual about
Virginia's Natural Bridge? ◆ How big is West Virginia's New
River Gorge Bridge? ◆ How did West Virginia become a
state? ◆ Why is Kentucky called the Bluegrass State? ◆ How
large is Mammoth Cave in Kentucky? ◆ How much gold is
stored at Fort Knox, Kentucky? ◆ Was there really once a
state named Franklin? ◆ What makes Reelfoot Lake in
Tennessee so unusual? ◆ How did the Smoky Mountains
get their name? ◆ What and where was the Lost Colony? ◆

CHAPTER 8

THE
SOUTH

State and Capital	Name Origin	Nickname	State Bird	State Flower	Land Area in Square Miles (sq km)	2000 Population
Virginia (Richmond)	After Queen Elizabeth I of England, the Virgin Queen	Old Dominion	Cardinal	Flowering dogwood	40,817 (106,124)	7,078,515
West Virginia (Charleston)	Was part of Virginia until Civil War	Mountain State	Cardinal	Rhododendron	24,181 (62,870)	1,808,344
Kentucky (Frankfort)	After Cherokee Indian word possibly meaning "land of tomorrow" or "meadowland"	Bluegrass State	Kentucky cardinal	Goldenrod	40,395 (105,027)	4,041,769
Tennessee (Nashville)	After the Cherokee Indian village Tanasie	Volunteer State	Mockingbird	Iris	42,244 (109,834)	5,689,283
North Carolina (Raleigh)	After King Charles I of England	Tar Heel State	Cardinal	Flowering dogwood	52,586 (136,724)	8,049,313
South Carolina (Columbia)	After King Charles I of England	Palmetto State	Carolina wren	Carolina jessamine	31,055 (80,743)	4,012,012
Georgia (Atlanta)	After King George II of England	Empire State of the South	Brown thrasher	Cherokee rose	58,876 (153,078)	8,186,453
Florida (Tallahassee)	Possibly for Spanish word florida, meaning "flowery"	Sunshine State	Mockingbird	Orange blossom	58,560 (152,256)	15,982,378

State and Capital	Name Origin	Nickname	State Bird	State Flower	Land Area in Square Miles (sq km)	2000 Population
Alabama (Montgomery)	After the Alibamu Indian tribe, meaning "I clear the thicket"	Heart of Dixie	Yellow-hammer	Camelia	51,609 (134,183)	4,447,100
Mississippi (Jackson)	After Indian word meaning "great water" or "father of waters"	Magnolia State	Mocking-bird	Magnolia	47,716 (124,062)	2,844,658
Louisiana, (Baton Rouge)	After French King Louis XIV	Pelican State	Brown pelican	Magnolia	48,523 (126,160)	4,468,976
Arkansas, (Little Rock)	French variant for the Quapaw Indians, meaning "down-stream people"	Land of Opportunity	Mocking-bird	Apple blossom	53,104 (138,070)	2,673,400

The southern states including capital cities. This region is known for its hot weather, but many areas regularly experience a frost and even some snow.

Washington, D.C.: A Planned City

The city of Washington was planned in detail before the first building was constructed—a rarity among world cities at that time. In the late 1700s, northern and southern leaders disagreed strongly about where to build a new permanent national capital, but they finally reached a compromise and agreed on a location along the Potomac River. The specific site for the District was selected by the first president, George Washington, in 1791. Maryland and Virginia contributed land for the new territory. It became the nation's capital in 1800, replacing Philadelphia.

Is the District of Columbia a state?

No, although many of its residents would like it to be. That's because they do not have a voting representative in the U.S. Congress, and because Congress has final authority over many aspects of their local government. Officially the District of Columbia is a territory of the United States, and the city of Washington occupies the entire 68-square-mile (177-sq-km) territory of the District of Columbia. About half a million people live there.

What else is on Capitol Hill besides the U.S. Capitol?

Capitol Hill is a rather low hill—only 88 feet (29 m) above sea level—near the center of Washington, D.C. The Capitol, which has 540 rooms, rises another 300 feet (91 m). It is surrounded by six congressional office buildings, the Library of Congress (which is the largest library in the world, housing more than 100 million books and other items), the U.S. Supreme Court building, and the U.S Botanic Garden. The Folger Shakespeare Library is also on Capitol Hill.

Why is Virginia called the Mother of States?

Virginia was the first American colony, dating back to 1584. For many years it was the largest colony and later the largest state in population. In the 1600s and 1700s Virginia consisted of huge amounts of land to the west,

Virginia is one of four states that call themselves commonwealths. The others are Pennsylvania, Kentucky, and Massachusetts. (See page 72 for more about commonwealths.)

The largest city in Virginia is not its capital, Richmond, but Virginia Beach. It had a 2000 population of 425,257, while Richmond's was 197,790. Richmond is Virginia's fourth-largest city—even Norfolk and Chesapeake are larger. Interestingly, the state capital is the largest city in only 17 of the 50 states.

extending all the way to the Mississippi River. This territory was later divided into the states of Illinois, Indiana, Kentucky, Michigan, Minnesota, Ohio, West Virginia, and Wisconsin.

Why is Virginia also known as the Mother of Presidents?

More U.S. presidents were born in Virginia than in any other state—eight. They were George Washington, Thomas Jefferson, James Madison, James Monroe, William Henry Harrison, John Tyler, Zachary Taylor, and Woodrow Wilson.

What's so unusual about Virginia's Natural Bridge?

The Natural Bridge, south of Lexington, Virginia, is a 90-foot (27-m)-wide, 215-foot (66-m)-high stone formation that really is a bridge—U.S. Route 11 runs directly over it. It was once part of a limestone cavern, but millions of years ago the soft rocks that made up the roof of the cavern collapsed. Some harder rocks were left standing,

Jamestown, Virginia: America's First Permanent English Settlement

Captain John Smith led a group of English colonists to establish a permanent settlement in America in May 1607. They chose a spot on a peninsula (which has since become an island) in the James River and named their community for King James I of England.

The settlers had a rough time from the start, and many died from disease and starvation in the first couple of years. If Lord De La Warr, Thomas West, hadn't arrived in nearby Hampton Roads in the nick of time in 1610, with plentiful supplies and a new group of settlers, Jamestown would have been abandoned. Several years later, the Jamestown colonists set up a representative form of government—the first on the North American continent—and began to grow tobacco as a trade crop to support themselves. Jamestown remained the seat of government in Virginia for almost ninety years, until Williamsburg took over the role in 1699.

The Natural Bridge in Virginia fascinated Thomas Jefferson, who was greatly interested in geography.

which formed the "bridge." Over millions of years, the stream that runs under the bridge carved away the bridge opening.

The first person to own the land surrounding the Natural Bridge was Thomas Jefferson, the third president. He was fascinated by this geological oddity and asked the royal governor of Virginia to grant him a tract of land that included the bridge in 1774. For many years he maintained a cabin there.

How big is West Virginia's New River Gorge Bridge?

The center span is 1,700 feet (518 m) long, making it the longest steel arch bridge in the world. Located near Fayetteville, the New River Gorge bridge took the title away from the Bayonne Bridge in New Jersey when it was completed in 1978. This bridge is also the second-highest bridge in the United States, rising 876 feet (267 m) over the New River Gorge. If you could place the Washington Monument under the bridge, you'd have 325 feet (99 m) to spare.

Contrary to its name, the New River is one of the oldest rivers in North America. The New River begins its northward flow near Boone, North Carolina, and then runs through Virginia and West Virginia. It joins with the Gauley River southeast of Charleston, West Virginia, to form the Kanawha River.

West Virginia provided most of the nation's bituminous coal throughout the twentieth century, but it contains another important resource— natural gas. Most of the west-central part of the state lies over huge natural gas fields.

How did West Virginia become a state?

Until 1863, the area that is now West Virginia was part of the state of Virginia. In 1861, at the beginning of the Civil War, most of the people living in the western part of Virginia did not want to secede from the Union with the rest of the state. For years the western Virginians had felt overlooked and poorly represented in the state legislature. In 1863 President Abraham Lincoln issued a presidential proclamation that made West Virginia the thirty-fifth state. It is the only state that was admitted to the Union in this way.

Why is Kentucky called the Bluegrass State?

The grass in the region around Lexington isn't really blue, but its blossoms are, giving the grass a blue tone when it is in bloom.

How large is Mammoth Cave in Kentucky?

At more than 350 miles (563 km) long, the Mammoth–Flint Ridge cave system in central Kentucky is the longest cave system in the world. Explorers are still discovering new passages. The cave was formed over the past 10 million years by slightly acidic rainwater filtering through the cracks of a limestone ridge, creating underground rivers that gradually carved out the cave. It features many interesting rock formations and several lakes, rivers, and waterfalls. Several types of blind animals live in the cave, including fish, beetles, and crayfish. Visitors can tour the cave at Mammoth Cave National Park.

How much gold is stored at Fort Knox, Kentucky?

More than $6 billion in gold bullion sits in vaults at Fort Knox. It is all owned by the federal government. The gold is stored as bars that are a little smaller than building bricks. Each bar contains about 400 troy ounces (12,441 g) of gold and weighs about 27.5 pounds (12.5 kg). The vault is so secure that during World War II the federal government sent their original copies of the U.S. Constitution and the Declaration of Independence to Fort Knox for safekeeping.

Was there really once a state named Franklin?

Yes, unofficially. For a short time, a part of what is now eastern Tennessee was known as Franklin, but it never officially became a U.S. state. Its founders, who were in such a remote region that they felt the need to band together to protect themselves, named their "state" for Benjamin Franklin. It existed between 1784 and 1790, when the federal government brought it into the newly formed Southwest Territory. Tennessee, including the area of Franklin, became an official U.S. state six years later.

What makes Reelfoot Lake in Tennessee so unusual?

This lake was created by fairly recent—geologically speaking—earthquakes. The huge New Madrid earthquakes of 1811 and 1812 (the strongest ever in the United States; see page 45 for more) caused a section of land near the Mississippi River in the northwestern corner of Tennessee to fall in. The waters of the Mississippi quickly rushed in to fill the hole. The lake is shallow—ranging between 2 and 9 feet (0.6 and 2.7 m) deep—but it is about 20 miles (32 km) long and 5 miles (8 km) wide. It is home to a large number of American bald eagles.

Many of the items we use every day—clothes and furniture in particular—come from North Carolina. Much of the wooden furniture sold in the United States is made there. North Carolina is also the nation's leading textile manufacturing state, with some 1,200 plants. The world's largest denim weaving mill is in Greensboro.

How did the Smoky Mountains get their name?

A bluish haze that looks like smoke often covers the mountains, also called the Smokies or Great Smokies. These mountains are part of the Appalachian Mountains and lie between Knoxville, Tennessee, and Asheville, North Carolina. The Appalachian Trail (see page 31) and the Blue Ridge Parkway both wind through these mountains. Some of the peaks reach 6,000 feet (1,823 m) and higher.

What and where was the Lost Colony?

The Lost Colony refers to one of the first groups of English settlers to come to America. The first group established a colony on Roanoke Island, off the North Carolina coast, in 1585, but they had a rough time and returned to England a year later. Another group came to the same spot in 1587. Its governor returned that year to England to get more supplies, and when he returned three years later everyone had disappeared—nearly a hundred people. No one has ever figured out what happened to them, although some think they may have moved to the Chesapeake Bay area but later died, possibly in fights with the Indians.

Hurricanes threaten North Carolina nearly every year. One of the worst to hit the state in recent years was Hurricane Floyd in 1999, causing severe flooding throughout the eastern part of the state and resulting in billions of dollars in damage.

Why is the area off Cape Hatteras, North Carolina, called the Graveyard of the Atlantic?

Cape Hatteras lies at the southeastern end of Hatteras Island, part of a string of 70 barrier islands that lie about 30 miles (48 km) east of the North Carolina coast. Over the past four centuries, at least 230 and perhaps as many as 2,200 ships have been wrecked in these waters because of storms, shoals, and dangerous currents. Especially treacherous are the shifting sand ridges called Diamond Shoals, in the shallow waters near the island.

Barrier islands are narrow islands of sand, silt, and gravel that lie parallel to coastlines. As sea levels have risen over the past several thousand years, Hatteras Island and other Outer Banks islands have become unstable. This is because storms cause tides to wash over them and move their sediments westward toward the coastline.

Moving the Cape Hatteras Lighthouse

The tallest lighthouse in the United States—the Cape Hatteras Lighthouse, at 210 feet (64 m) above sea level—had to be moved inland in 1999 to save it from falling into the sea.

Now the landmark rests a safe 1,600 feet (488 m) from the Atlantic Ocean. When it was built in 1870, it stood 1,500 feet (457 m) from the ocean, but by 1935 so much erosion had occurred that the structure was less than 100 feet (305 m) from the water. To move the lighthouse, engineers had to remove the old granite base and replace it with steel support towers. Hydraulic jacks lifted the lighthouse 6 feet (1.8 m) into the air and placed it on steel support beams. Hydraulic jacks were also used to push the lighthouse along rollers until it was 2,900 feet (884 m) inland. There it was placed on a new concrete foundation.

How did North Carolina come to be called the Tar Heel State?

One of the state's earliest products was tar. The term "tar heel" is said to have come from North Carolina soldiers who were left to fight a Civil War battle alone, after other members of the Confederate forces retreated. The North Carolinians said they would put tar on the heels of those who retreated so they would "stick better in the next fight."

It's easy to get confused by town names in the Carolinas. Both North Carolina and South Carolina have towns named Greenville, Beaufort, Jacksonville, Tarboro, Williamston, Camden, and Black River.

The Carolina and Georgia Sand Hills

A series of ancient beaches and sand dunes called sand hills—some of them 30 miles (48 km) wide—runs from southwestern Georgia across central South Carolina and into south-central North Carolina. The sand was left behind millions of years ago by a receding sea. The sand hills are quite deep and cover 8,760 square miles (22,779 sq km) across those three states. Even though the region gets plenty of rain, the sand doesn't retain moisture well, so the sand hills area is considered semiarid. The Carolina sand hills are sometimes called "deserts in the rain."

Nearly half of all Georgia residents live in the Atlanta metropolitan area.

What is Georgia known for producing besides peaches?

Georgia, which is the largest state in land area east of the Mississippi River, is the leading U.S. producer of peanuts, which Georgians call goobers. Pecans are another important crop. Georgia also has large deposits of marble, and marble slabs from quarries there have been used to build several state capitol buildings and portions of the Lincoln Memorial in Washington, D.C.

Before the California Gold Rush in the 1840s, there was the Georgia Gold Rush in the 1830s. Gold was discovered in the area around Dahlonega, and for a while it was the nation's major source of gold.

What and where is the Rock Eagle effigy in Georgia?

It is an ancient Indian sculpture depicting a large bird that was found near Eatonton, Georgia. Anthropologists think it is about 6,000 years old and was used in religious ceremonies. It was carved onto a milky white quartz rock and measures 102 feet (31 m) from head to tail and 120 feet (37 m) from wingtip to wingtip. Similar rock effigies have been found throughout the South.

How did Stone Mountain in Georgia form?

Stone Mountain is a 700-foot (213-m)-high dome-shaped granite hill near Atlanta, Georgia. It is thought to be the largest mass of exposed granite in the world, measuring about 2 miles (3.2 km) long and 1 mile (1.6 km) wide. It was formed 300 million years ago when hot liquid rock, called magma, approached the Earth's surface and later hardened. Eventually the land on top of the rock eroded or washed away and left the top of the rock exposed.

Granite was quarried here until 1978. Today Stone Mountain is a state park, and visitors come to see the world's largest relief carving on one side—a memorial to the South's Civil War heroes, including Jefferson Davis, Robert E. Lee, and Stonewall Jackson.

Even though Stone Mountain reminds some people of Ayers Rock in Australia, these two rock outcroppings differ in several ways. Ayers Rock is made up of sandstone and is much larger—it rises more than 1,100 feet (335 m) high and is about 11 miles (18 km) long and 1 mile (1.6 km) wide.

Why is Florida one of the fastest-growing states in the nation?

Florida is the fourth most populous state. In 1980 it had 9.7 million people; about 16 million people live there today. One reason for its popularity is its warm year-round climate, which makes it an attractive retirement destination for people who no longer want to put up with cold, snow, and ice. Also, the cost of living is lower there than in many parts of the country.

How far is Florida from Cuba at its closest point?

The southern tip of the state is less than 100 miles (161 km) from the island nation of Cuba. Ever since Cuba became a Communist nation in the early 1960s, some of its citizens have tried to escape political oppression by sailing on small boats to the United States. Many Cubans have settled in the cities of Miami and Hialeah and have become American citizens.

Does most of the orange juice we drink come from Florida?

Yes; almost all the orange juice we drink is processed in Florida. The state grows 80 percent of all oranges and grapefruit in the United States.

Is St. Augustine, Florida, the oldest city in the United States?

Yes. St. Augustine was founded in 1565 by a Spanish explorer, Pedro Menendez de Aviles. It is more than 40 years older than either Santa Fe, New Mexico, or Jamestown, Virginia. Florida belonged to Spain until 1821, when the U.S. government bought it.

What are the Everglades?

The Everglades are swampy grasslands that cover southern Florida. Everglades National Park, which covers only a fifth of the Everglades region, was established to preserve this unusual ecosystem—for example, it is the only place in the world where alligators and crocodiles live together. The park covers 2,342 square miles (6,090 sq km). It is also a World Heritage Site, an International Biosphere Reserve, and a Wetland of International Importance.

All of the state of Florida is south of the state of California.

The Everglades are now thought of as swamps, but a hundred years ago this watery area was a river 50 miles (81 km) wide and only 6 inches (15 cm) deep. It flowed from Lake Okeechobee to the Florida Bay. As people moved into this part of southern Florida, engineers interrupted the flow of the river by adding dikes, canals, and pipes to provide water to farms and homes.

The Everglades are in danger today for several reasons, primarily because their water supply has been threatened. The region depends on rainfall, but human activities in the surrounding areas siphon off much of the water before it can reach the park. Pollutants are also entering the area, causing damage to vegetation and disruption to the food chain. Mercury poisoning has killed at least one of the endangered Florida panthers there, a tragedy because there are probably fewer than 30 panthers left in the state.

What are the Florida Keys?

Key is another way of spelling cay (they're pronounced the same way) from the Spanish word *cayo,* which means a small island made up largely of coral or sand. The Florida Keys stretch from Biscayne Bay southwestward off the southern tip of the state for about 150 miles (242 km). Key Largo is the largest, and Key West is the most distant from Miami.

To get to Key West from Miami, you must travel nearly 160 miles (258 km), mostly on U.S Route 1, the

The Florida Keys are connected via U.S. Route 1, which runs on numerous long bridges over the shallow waters separating the islands.

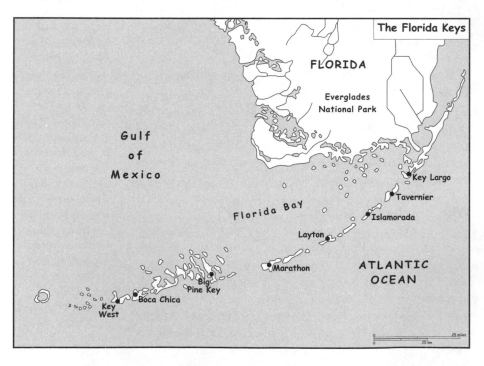

Overseas Highway. This road takes you across 42 bridges as it hops from island to island.

What's that huge body of water in the southern part of Florida?

That is Lake Okeechobee, Florida's largest lake. It is second only to Lake Michigan as the largest body of fresh-water wholly within U.S. boundaries. It covers about 680 square miles (1,768 sq km). Like Wisconsin, Florida can be called a land of lakes—some 30,000 shallow lakes are found in central Florida.

What is a bayou?

Bayous are common sights in the southern states. They are shallow, marshy creeks found in flat areas with poor drainage. The Mobile Delta in southern Alabama has many swamps and bayous.

Why is most of the soil in Alabama and other places in the South so red?

Color is one way geologists classify soil. Red soil can mean that there are iron oxides present—the case in Alabama and much of the South. In places that are hot and wet for much of the year, like Hawaii, red soil can indicate that water has removed much of the nutrients (a process called leaching), leaving behind very infertile soils.

Little River in Alabama is the only river in the United States that runs entirely across the top of a mountain. It flows on Lookout Mountain in the northeastern part of the state.

What is the ivylike plant that covers so much of the South, especially in Mississippi?

The plant that smothers millions of acres of the South is kudzu, and it is not native to the United States. It was first seen in the United States at the 1876 Centennial Exposition in Philadelphia, where the Japanese planted it in a garden. It became popular in the South, and it was widely used to control erosion on hillsides in the 1930s. Kudzu can grow as much as 60 feet (18 m) a year. Unfortunately, it may take years to get rid of, even with the most effective herbicides.

What is the Emerald Mound, along the Natchez Parkway in Mississippi?

Emerald Mound is the remains of a ceremonial mound built about 700 years ago by Native Americans. It was part of a town that once sat here, one of many similar settlements in the Mississippi Delta area. It stands 35 feet (11 m) high and covers 8 acres (3.2 ha). A fairly advanced civilization that scientists call the Mississippians lived in the Southeast, building roads, villages, mounds, and other structures. In about 1450 the civilization declined for unknown reasons.

Is the city of Texarkana in Texas or Arkansas?

It straddles the border of these states. Although it has two city governments, one in each state, it has just one post office. Its address reads "Texarkana, Arkansas-Texas."

Are there any diamond mines in the United States?

Yes, just one—in Murfreesboro, Arkansas. Visitors can hunt for and keep any diamonds they find there.

How hot are the Hot Springs in Arkansas?

They're really hot—about 143° Fahrenheit. The world-famous Hot Springs in the Ouachita Mountains are made up of 47 separate springs that put out about 1 million gallons (3.8 million l) of steaming water a day. Hot Springs is now a national park, but back in the early 1800s people began coming to Hot Springs to "take the waters" for health reasons. Springs are places in the earth where water flows to the surface from underneath the earth. The water in hot or warm springs is heated as it travels past hot rocks deep in our planet.

Other famous Arkansas springs are Mammoth Spring, which is one of the largest in the United States, and Eureka Springs, both in the Ozarks.

How far can a ship travel up the Mississippi River from the Gulf of Mexico?

Small ships can make it up the Mississippi from New Orleans all the way to Minneapolis, Minnesota, about

1,800 miles (2,898 km) north. The river is 9 to 100 feet (2.7 to 31 m) deep most of the way, and at one point—north of Clinton, Iowa—it is 3.5 miles (5.6 km) wide.

Which U.S. city has the busiest port?

The Port of South Louisiana, outside New Orleans, Louisiana, is the nation's busiest port and the world's third busiest, when measured by tonnage handled. The port is huge, extending 54 miles (87 km) along the Mississippi River. More than 4,000 oceangoing vessels call there each year. Most shipments leaving the port are corn, wheat, and soybeans. The next busiest ports, in order, are Houston, Texas; New York, New York; New Orleans, Louisiana; and Baton Rouge, Louisiana.

What's the difference between Creole and Cajun?

In Louisiana, Creoles are people who generally live in the southern part of the state whose ancestors were among the original French and Spanish settlers. Cajuns are those whose ancestors came from the Acadia region of eastern Canada. The French and Spanish influence in Louisiana continues today and is reflected in the traditional foods of the region.

Is it true that New Orleans is sinking?

Yes, and some scientists are predicting that the city could be underwater within a century. Today more than two-thirds of the city is already about 8 feet (2.4 m) below sea level. This sinking, or subsidence, is happening because the city was built on the soft silt of the Mississippi Delta.

To make matters worse, the surrounding marshlands and low-lying barrier islands that have protected the city from hurricane damage in the past are also sinking. And if predictions about global warming and rising sea levels come to pass, the loss of land to the sea will take place even sooner. Each year 25 square miles (65 sq km) of land are lost to the water. Geologists are looking at possible solutions. One is to build a 25-foot (7.6-m)-high wall across the southern part of the city.

An ample source of fresh water and sediment, the Mississippi shaped much of the coastline of Louisiana. Today, the effects of human and natural forces on the river's course place the coastal wetlands at risk.

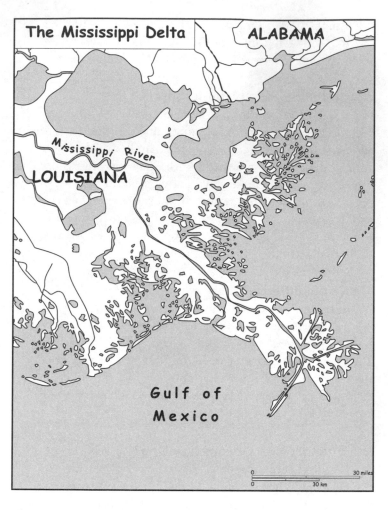

The Mississippi Delta

ALABAMA

Mississippi River

LOUISIANA

Gulf of Mexico

0   30 miles
0   30 km

What is the Mississippi Delta?

A delta is a flat plain that often lies at the mouth of a river. It is created when a river slows as it enters a lake or an ocean, leaving behind deposits of silt, clay, sand, and gravel, which taken together are called alluvium.

The Mississippi Delta is called a bird-foot delta because several channels branch off the main channel, giving the appearance of a bird's foot when viewed from above. The Mississippi Delta grows by about 200 million tons (182 million metric tn) of sediment each year. Today it covers about 13,000 square miles (33,800 sq km), or about a fourth of Louisiana's total land area.

What are the salt domes off the Louisiana shore?

More than 500 salt domes have been discovered along the Gulf Coast, from Texas to the Florida panhandle. They are mostly made of pure salt, or halite, and were formed over millions of years from thick beds of salt several miles below the Earth's surface. Because the salt walls will not allow fluid or gas to escape, some of the domes are ideal for storing petroleum products such as propane, butane, ethane, and methane.

The U.S. government stores an emergency supply of crude oil in more than 50 of these salt domes along the Texas and Louisiana coast. It is called the Strategic Petroleum Reserve, and with a capacity of 700 million gallons (2.6 trillion l) is the largest emergency stockpile in the world. A typical salt dome cavern is 200 feet (61 m) in diameter, 2,000 feet (610 m) high—tall enough for Chicago's Sears Tower to fit inside with room to spare—and can hold up to 10 million barrels of oil.

If you like crayfish, Louisiana is the place to be. The state produces more crayfish than any other place in the world. Most are raised in crayfish farms using a method called aquaculture (see page 84 for more about aquaculture).

CHAPTER 9

THE SOUTHWEST

Do many Native Americans still live in Oklahoma? ◆ How did Oklahomans come to be called Sooners? ◆ What's unusual about the state capitol building in Oklahoma City? ◆ How many different national flags have flown over Texas? ◆ How much land does Texas have compared with some other states? ◆ What is the large barrier island that runs along the South Texas coast? ◆ How big is the King Ranch in Texas? ◆ Is all of Texas flat? ◆ Which state has the highest average altitude—Alaska or Colorado? ◆ What is the Garden of the Gods, near Colorado Springs? ◆ Is Denver, Colorado, in the Rocky Mountains? ◆ How large is Carlsbad Caverns in New Mexico? ◆ Are there any volca

State and Capital	Name Origin	Nickname	State Bird	State Flower	Land Area in Square Miles (sq km)	2000 Population
Oklahoma (Oklahoma City)	From Choctaw Indian words *okla,* meaning "people" and *homma,* meaning "red"	Sooner State	Scissor-tailed flycatcher	Mistletoe	69,919 (181,789)	3,450,654
Texas (Austin)	From Indian word *tejas*	Lone Star State	Mocking-bird	Bluebonnet	267,338 (695,079)	20,851,820
Colorado (Denver)	From the Spanish word *colorado,* meaning "colored red"	Centennial State	Lark bunting	Rocky Mountain columbine	104,247 (271,042)	4,301,261
New Mexico (Santa Fe)	Named by Spanish to refer to land north and west of Rio Grande	Land of Enchantment	Road-runner	Yucca flower	121,666 (316,332)	1,819,046
Arizona (Phoenix)	After Indian word possibly meaning "small spring"	Grand Canyon State	Cactus wren	Saguaro cactus	113,909 (296,163)	5,130,632

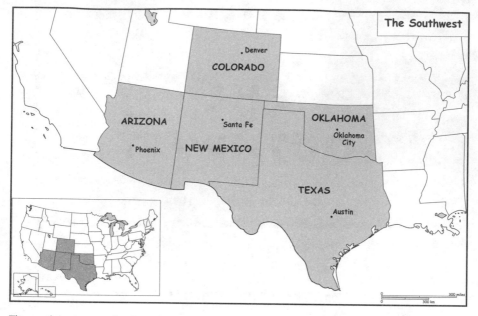

The southwestern states including capital cities. This region is marked by its Hispanic history and vibrant culture, as well as its deserts, mountains, and plains.

There are more man-made lakes in Oklahoma than in any other state. Combined, these lakes have more than 1 million surface acres (400,000 ha) of water.

Do many Native Americans still live in Oklahoma?

Oklahoma is home to about 272,000 Native Americans, who make up almost 8 percent of the population. Many are descended from the 67 tribes that lived there when the state was Indian Territory. These tribes included the Cherokee, Choctaw, Chickasaw, Creek, Seminole, Osage, Cheyenne, Sac and Fox, Delaware, Apache, and Pawnee.

How did Oklahomans come to be called Sooners?

Back in 1889, on the first day people were allowed to lay claim to free government land there, some of the 50,000 eager settlers tried to stake their claims before the noon starting gun. They were called Sooners—they arrived a little too soon.

The U.S. government purchased this land, about 3 million acres (1.2 million ha), from the Creek and Seminole Native American tribes.

What's unusual about the state capitol building in Oklahoma City?

It's the only capitol building in the world to have a working oil well on the grounds. The well is often called Petunia No. 1 because it was drilled into a flowerbed after the capitol was built. The capitol building itself is also a little unusual because the state is finally building a dome on it. Most state capitols were built with domes similar to the one on the U.S. Capitol.

How many different national flags have flown over Texas?

Six. At various times in its history, parts of the area that now form the state of Texas belonged at different times to Spain, France, and Mexico—its first three flags. After gaining independence from Mexico in 1836, Texas became an independent nation, the Republic of Texas, and flew a flag of its own—number four. Then the state joined the Union in 1845 and flew the American flag—number five. When Texas seceded from the Union during the Civil War to become part of the Confederate States of America, it flew the Confederate flag—number six.

Only two state capitals include the state name in their name. One is Oklahoma City, Oklahoma, and the other is Indianapolis, Indiana.

How much land does Texas have compared with some other states?

It's the second-largest state in total area (land and water combined), after Alaska. Texas contains 267,277 square miles (694,920 sq km), but Alaska is much larger, with 615,230 square miles (1,599,598 sq km). Put another way, Texas is bigger than the six New England states plus New York, Pennsylvania, North Carolina, and Ohio combined.

Car trips across the state can take a while. If you were to cross the state from near El Paso in the west to a point in Nelson County in the east, you'd travel 773 miles (1,245 km). To go from the northernmost point in the Texas panhandle to the southernmost tip near Brownsville, you'd drive 801 miles (1,290 km).

Even though Texas ranks second (behind California) in population and has 3 of the 10 largest U.S. cities (Dallas, Houston, and San Antonio), the state has about the same number of people as the New York City metropolitan area.

What is the large barrier island that runs along the South Texas coast?

It's Padre Island, one of the last undeveloped barrier islands in the world. That's because the U.S. National Park Service has designated nearly 70 miles (113 km) of the 130-mile (209-km) island as Padre Island National Seashore.

Barrier islands are one of four basic types of islands; the others are continental, oceanic, and coral. Barrier

Padre Island National Seashore is a clear example of a barrier island formation. Such formations are prone to severe damage and reshaping in hurricanes and storms.

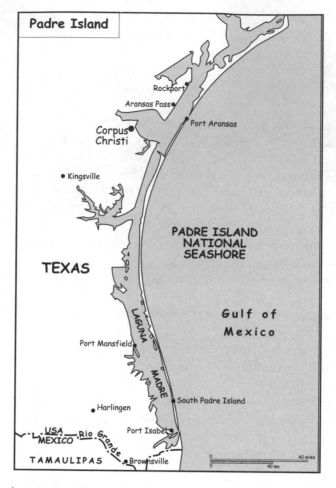

Padre Island

Rockport
Aransas Pass
Port Aransas
Corpus Christi
Kingsville
PADRE ISLAND NATIONAL SEASHORE
TEXAS
Gulf of Mexico
LAGUNA
Port Mansfield
MADRE
Harlingen
South Padre Island
USA
MEXICO Rio Grande
Port Isabel
TAMAULIPAS   Brownsville
0   40 miles
0   40 km

The shortest river in Texas is the Comal River, at only 2.5 miles (4 km) long. Crystal clear, the Comal originates from a spring in the central Texas town of New Braunfels and empties into the Guadalupe River in that same town.

islands run parallel to coastlines, and the water that lies between them and the mainland is called a lagoon or a sound. They're called barrier islands because their sand dunes tend to protect the main coastline from powerful winds and waves.

How big is the King Ranch in Texas?

The King Ranch—one of the largest working ranches in the world—covers 1,300 square miles (3,380 sq km), an area bigger than Rhode Island. The ranch is located between Corpus Christi and Brownsville. Even though it is best known as a cattle ranch, with 60,000 cattle, the King Ranch is also a very large 60,000-acre (24,000-ha) farm that grows cotton and grain sorghum.

Texas Firsts

Texas leads the nation in several ways. It produces more cotton than any other state. It produces more beef cattle and sheep than any other state. And it produces more oil and natural gas than any other state (it contains a fourth of the nation's proved oil reserves). Pipelines deliver Texas natural gas to states as far away as New York.

Is all of Texas flat?

Yes, most parts of the state are quite flat. But in a part of West Texas called the Trans-Pecos region, west of the Pecos River, the terrain is mountainous. In fact, eight mountains in the Guadalupe range have elevations of more than 8,000 feet (2,438 m) above sea level.

Which state has the highest average altitude— Alaska or Colorado?

Colorado, which has an average elevation of 6,800 feet (2,073 m). Alaska's average elevation is just 1,900 feet (579 m). This is because many parts of Alaska lie at or near sea level. But the lowest spot in Colorado is still 3,350 feet (1,021 m) above sea level, near the town of Holly on the Arkansas River.

The highest peak in Colorado is Mount Elbert, one of many high mountains in the Sawatch range of the Rocky Mountains. It rises 14,433 feet (4,402 m), or 2.73 miles (4.4 km), above sea level. Colorado has 53 mountains that reach more than 14,000 feet (4,267 m) above sea level, and 831 that rise between 11,000 feet (3,353 m) and 14,000 feet (4,267 m).

What is the Garden of the Gods, near Colorado Springs?

The Garden of the Gods is the name of a city park that features a natural collection of dramatically shaped red sandstone rock formations. Many rocks in the state are a reddish color, so it makes sense that the name "Colorado" comes from the Spanish word *colorado,* which means "colored red."

The world's highest suspension bridge over water is the Royal Gorge Bridge, over the Arkansas River near Canon City, Colorado. Built in 1929 using wood and steel, the bridge is 1,053 feet (321 m) high and one-quarter mile (.4 km) long.

A huge "nugget" of silver weighing 1,840 pounds (828 kg)—the largest ever found in the United States—was uncovered in the seventh level of the Smuggler Mine near Aspen, Colorado, in 1894.

Denver, the capital of Colorado, is called the Mile High City because of its altitude above sea level. Surveyors have marked the exact spot, at 5,280 feet (8,500 m), on the sixteenth step of the state capitol building.

Is Denver, Colorado, in the Rocky Mountains?

Not quite—the mountains begin to rise about 15 miles (24 km) west of Denver, which lies on fairly flat land. Even so, the city sits 1 mile (1.6 m) above sea level, just because the land itself is so elevated because of the nearby mountainous terrain.

Denver became a settlement after the first gold in Colorado was discovered there in 1858. The gold is long gone, but the city has since become a major business and transportation hub.

How large is Carlsbad Caverns in New Mexico?

Carlsbad Caverns has three major levels, the deepest of which is more than 1,000 feet (305 m) under the earth. Explorers have mapped 30 miles (48 km) of caves and corridors in the main cavern, 3 miles (5 km) of which are open to visitors. The Big Room features a 255-foot (78-m)-high ceiling and a stalagmite called the Giant Dome, which is 62 feet (19 m) tall. The caverns are part of Carlsbad Caverns National Park, which also protects 86 other caves in the Guadalupe Mountains area.

Are there any volcanoes in New Mexico?

There are no active volcanoes, but Capulin Mountain is an impressive example of an extinct volcano that blew its top about 62,000 years ago—quite recently from a geologist's point of view. It stands 8,182 feet (2,494 m) above sea level and rises about 1,300 feet (396 m) above the surrounding plain. Other extinct volcanoes and ancient lava flows in the region remind us that this region was once a violent place.

Capulin Mountain is one of the few extinct volcanoes in the world that visitors can walk into.

What is the river that forms the U.S. boundary with Mexico?

About two-thirds of the border between the United States and Mexico is marked by the Rio Grande. In all, the Rio Grande is 1,760 miles (2,834 km) long. It begins as a stream high in Colorado's Rocky Mountains and travels through New Mexico and Texas into the Gulf of Mexico. Along the way, its waters help irrigate 2 million acres (0.8 million ha) of farmland in the United States and Mexico. It is the fifth-longest river in North America and the twentieth-longest in the world.

It's redundant to say "Rio Grande River" because *río* means "river" in Spanish. People in Mexico have another name for it: Río Bravo del Norte.

Santa Fe, the capital of New Mexico, is the oldest seat of government in the United States. It was founded to serve as the capital of a Spanish province around 1610.

What is the meaning of the sunlike design on the New Mexico state flag?

The design features a red *zia* on a field of gold. The zia symbolizes the Sun and reflects the beliefs of the ancient Zia Pueblo Indians. They believed that four was a sacred number, and each of the four sets of four lines radiating from the center circle represent aspects of life on Earth.

Which southwestern states meet at Four Corners?

Arizona, New Mexico, Colorado, and Utah. You can get to this unique spot by taking U.S. 160 in Arizona.

How big is the Grand Canyon?

The Grand Canyon, located in the northwestern corner of Arizona, stretches more than 277 miles (446 km). It is more than 1 mile (1.6 km) deep in places and about 18 miles (29 km) wide at its widest point. This amazing gash in the earth was cut by the powerful flow of the Colorado River beginning about 6 million years ago. Geologists can learn a lot about the ancient history of this region by studying the many layers of rock that the river has exposed.

The federal government owns or controls about 70 percent of Arizona's land.

How did the Petrified Forest form?

More than 225 million years ago, trees then growing in this part of northeastern Arizona were buried in volcanic ash, mud, or sand and eventually turned to stone. Today the area, within the Painted Desert—another colorful part of Arizona—contains one of the world's largest concentrations of petrified wood.

Tucson, Arizona: Astronomy Capital of the World

The mountain peaks around Tucson have the largest concentration of telescopes anywhere in the world. About 30 optical telescopes—including those at Lowell Observatory and Kitt Peak National Observatory—study the stars and planets from this part of the Arizona desert, where dark night skies and dry desert air give astronomers good views of the stars.

Even Rome's Vatican Observatory, one of the oldest astronomical institutes in the world, operates a research center at the University of Arizona. It came to Arizona because the Italian skies near Rome became too bright for nighttime viewing.

Tucson is beginning to face the same problem as the city grows, and astronomers are beginning to complain about light pollution—the light given off by homes, businesses, and streetlights. As a result, local governments have passed ordinances limiting outdoor lighting levels by businesses.

CHAPTER 10

Why is Montana called the Treasure State? ◆ How many glaciers are there at Glacier National Park in Montana? ◆ What is a glacier? ◆ What makes Montana's rivers unique among the 50 states? ◆ What does "Idaho" mean? ◆ Is it true that Idaho has a seaport? ◆ What can you see at Craters of the Moon National Monument in southeastern Idaho? ◆ Why is Idaho called the Gem State? ◆ Why is Wyoming called the Equality State? ◆ Is Yellowstone National Park in Wyoming? ◆ What are geysers, fumaroles, mudpots, and hot springs? ◆ Why is the Great Salt Lake in Utah so salty? ◆ Why did the Mormons settle in Utah? ◆ Why is the seagull the state bird of Utah? ◆ Why is Utah

THE WEST

State and Capital	Name Origin	Nickname	State Bird	State Flower	Land Area in Square Miles (sq km)	2000 Population
Montana (Helena)	From Spanish word meaning "mountainous"	Treasure State	Western meadow-lark	Bitterroot	147,138 (382,559)	902,195
Idaho (Boise)	Coined word	Gem State	Mountain bluebird	Syringa	83,557 (217,248)	1,293,953
Wyoming (Cheyenne)	After Delaware Indian word meaning "upon the great plain"	Equality State	Meadow-lark	Indian paintbrush	97,914 (254,576)	493,782
Utah (Salt Lake City)	Named by U.S. Congress after Ute Indian tribe	Beehive State	Seagull	Sego lily	84,916 (220,782)	2,233,169
Nevada (Carson City)	From Spanish word meaning "snowclad"	Silver State	Mountain bluebird	Sagebrush	110,540 (287,404)	1,998,257
California (Sacramento)	Named by Spanish explorers after a fictitious island	Golden State	California valley quail	Golden poppy	158,869 (413,059)	33,871,648
Hawaii (Honolulu)	From native Hawaiian word or words meaning "homeland"	Aloha State	Nene	Yellow hibiscus	6,450 (16,770)	1,211,537

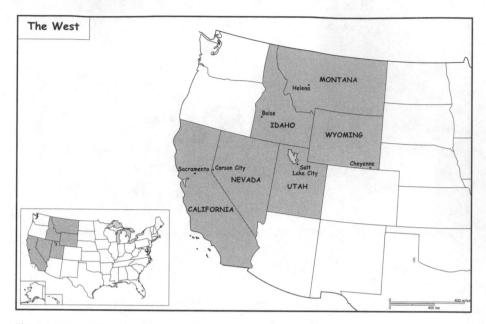

The West

The western states including capital cities. This area includes some of the fastest growing states in the nation—Nevada and Utah—as well as some of the least populous—Montana and Wyoming.

Montana is the fourth-largest state in land area, after Alaska, Texas, and California.

Why is Montana called the Treasure State?

Because early settlers found a wealth of gold and silver in its mountains.

How many glaciers are there at Glacier National Park in Montana?

Glacier National Park features more than 50 glaciers and 200 lakes and streams in its 1.4 million mountainous acres (560,000 ha).

What is a glacier?

A glacier is an accumulation of snow that forms when more snow falls each winter than melts the following summer. As the layers grow year after year, their weight causes the lower layers to compress and turn into a dense ice called firn. When this ice begins to move slowly over the land or down a mountainside, it becomes a glacier. Glaciers have carved out many of the world's lakes and mountains over the eons.

The glaciers in Glacier National Park are only a few thousand years old, which is relatively young in geological terms. They are slowly shrinking in size because more of their snow melts each summer than accumulates each winter.

Insects on Ice

Grasshopper Glacier, near Cooke City, Montana, is a most unusual natural phenomenon: huge swarms of grasshoppers have been trapped in the ice of a glacier for more than 300 years. This oddity was discovered in 1898 during a scientific expedition in the northern Rockies near Granite Peak, not far from Yellowstone National Park.

One of the scientists noticed a strange-looking section of ice with a surface that looked like elephant skin. When he got closer, he saw that its unusual appearance was caused by hundreds of dead bugs locked inside. Scientists think that the insects may have been flying over the area when they were caught in a storm.

What makes Montana's rivers unique among the 50 states?

Montana's rivers flow into three widely separated bodies of water: the Gulf of Mexico, the Pacific Ocean, and the Hudson Bay. The Missouri River system drains into the Mississippi River and then into the Gulf of Mexico; the Columbia River system drains into the Pacific Ocean; and the Belly, St. Mary's, and Waterton Rivers drain into Hudson Bay by way of the Nelson and Saskatchewan Rivers system.

The first woman to be elected to the U.S. House of Representatives was from Montana. Her name was Jeanette Rankin, and she was elected in 1916.

What does "Idaho" mean?

Nothing at all! It is a coined—or made-up—word, not a Native American word. It was suggested by a man in 1860 to be the name for the Colorado Territory, but people didn't like it because it *wasn't* a Native American word. Two years later, the name was used for a new western territory, part of which later became the state of Idaho.

The Idaho town of Island Park claims to have the longest main street in the United States. It is 33 miles (53 km) long.

Is it true that Idaho has a seaport?

Lewiston, Idaho, sometimes called the Seaport of Idaho, is really a riverport at the confluence of the Snake and Clearwater Rivers. Boats and barges carry farm and forest products down to the Columbia River and through neighboring Washington State to the Pacific Ocean, a

The Thousand Springs area of Idaho's Hagerman Valley, in the Snake River Canyon, produces more than 80 percent of all the commercial fresh and frozen rainbow trout sold in the United States.

journey of 465 miles (749 km). Lewiston was one of Idaho's first cities and was named for the early American explorer Meriwether Lewis, of Lewis and Clark expedition fame.

What can you see at Craters of the Moon National Monument in southeastern Idaho?

This 83-square-mile (216-sq-km) area is a basaltic lava field created by more than 15,000 years of volcanic activity. Visitors can view many interesting volcanic features, such as lava tubes, several types of lava flows, cinder cones, and spatter cones. In the 1960s this area was used to train the astronauts for the Apollo moon landings.

Why is Idaho called the Gem State?

Because it produces 72 different types of precious and semiprecious gemstones, including star garnets, opals, jade, and agate.

Why is Wyoming called the Equality State?

The Wyoming territorial constitution was the first constitution in the world to give women full voting rights, back in 1889. It became a U.S. state a year later. Wyoming also claims the first woman governor in the United States, Nellie Tayloe Ross, who was elected in 1925 to replace her husband, who had died while in office. In 1933 she became the first woman to head the U.S. Mint.

Keeping Warm in Boise

Idaho's state capitol building in Boise is heated by pumping up naturally hot water from 3,000 feet (914 m) below the Earth. This form of energy is called geothermal. The water is warmed by heat coming from underground chambers of magma, or molten rock. (Magma produces lava during a volcanic eruption.) In areas of volcanic activity, magma lies near the surface, making geothermal energy systems possible. Many homes and businesses in Iceland, for example, depend on geothermal heat.

Is Yellowstone National Park in Wyoming?

Yes, mostly, but parts of the 2.2-million-acre (880,000-ha) park are also in Idaho and Montana. Yellowstone National Park was the first national park when it was established in 1872. The park is unusual in that it contains half of the world's geothermal features. It has more than 300 geysers (two-thirds the world's total, including Old Faithful), and more than 10,000 hot springs, mudpots, and fumaroles.

What are geysers, fumaroles, mudpots, and hot springs?

Geysers are bursts of boiling hot water that erupt from below the surface into the air, often several hundred feet. A fumarole is a steam vent. The steam comes from hot springs below the Earth's surface that are so hot that their water boils away before they reach the surface.

A mudpot looks like it sounds—a hot, bubbling mound of clay and sand mixed with a little water. It smells like rotten eggs because it contains sulfuric acid. Hot springs occur when water below the Earth's surface passes across hot rocks in areas of recent (geologically speaking) volcanic activity and then flows to the surface of the Earth.

Why is the Great Salt Lake in Utah so salty?

Water from freshwater streams flows into the Great Salt Lake, but it never flows back out. When it evaporates, salt (sodium chloride) and other minerals are left behind, making the water salty. The amount of salt in the lake varies, depending on how much water is present. The southern section contains 5 to 14 percent salt and the northern section about 16 to 27 percent salt. In comparison, ocean water is about 3.5 percent salt. If you go swimming in the lake, you'll float quite easily. Don't plan on going fishing, though; fish can't survive in such salty conditions, although brine shrimp live there.

In dry weather the lake can shrink in size because much of the water evaporates. On average, the Great Salt Lake is about 75 miles (121 km) long and 30 miles (48 km) wide.

Wyoming ranks last in population of all the states—even Alaska has more people. On average, there are only five people per square mile in Wyoming. In contrast, there are 1,094 people per square mile in New Jersey.

Geologists believe that the Great Salt Lake was once part of a huge ancient freshwater lake they call Lake Bonneville. Today, at the international speedway on the Bonneville Salt Flats—part of the dried-up bed of that ancient lake—race cars have set world speed records, with some vehicles exceeding 600 miles per hour (966 km/hr).

Why did the Mormons settle in Utah?

Back in New York in 1830, a man named Joseph Smith established the Church of Jesus Christ of Latter-day Saints. Over the next 20 years, the church spread to Ohio, Missouri, and Illinois, but everywhere they went, its members were persecuted by people of other denominations.

In 1847 they decided to travel west to find a place where they could practice their beliefs freely. Led by Brigham Young, 148 Latter-Day Saints reached Utah and built a settlement near the Great Salt Lake. They found peace there because no one else wanted to live in such a desolate place. Today, 70 percent of the people living in Utah are Mormons, and the church has spread around the world.

Why is the seagull the state bird of Utah?

Back in 1848, Utah was invaded by millions of Rocky Mountain crickets that began destroying crops and threatening the people with starvation. Seemingly out of nowhere, flocks of California gulls appeared and began eating the crickets. The people were so grateful that more than a hundred years later this species of gull was selected as the official state bird. Seagulls don't always live near the sea. Many species, including California gulls, live primarily on inland lakes.

Why is Utah called the Beehive State?

Utahans selected the beehive as their official state emblem because honeybees represent the virtues of industry and perseverance. A drawing of a beehive appears on its state flag and state seal, as well as on its state highway signs. The early Mormon settlers wanted the Utah Territory to be called "Deseret," which means "honeybee" in the Book of Mormon.

Utah also chose the honeybee as its official state insect. It is not alone—15 other states also selected the honeybee as their state insect: Arkansas, Georgia, Kansas, Louisiana, Maine, Mississippi, Missouri, Nebraska, New Jersey, North Carolina, Oklahoma, South Dakota, Tennessee, Vermont, and Wisconsin.

What's the driest state in the United States?

Nevada receives less rain than any other state. Rainfall in the southeastern part of the state averages only about 4 inches (10 cm) a year. But Nevada has plenty of water in Lake Mead, which stretches for about 115 miles (185 km), one of the largest artificially created lakes in the world.

Lake Mead was formed when the Hoover Dam was built on the Colorado River at the Nevada-Arizona border, east of Las Vegas, in the 1930s. It is the highest concrete arch dam in the nation, rising 726 feet (221 m). A power plant at the dam generates electricity for Arizona, California, and Nevada.

Why do the words "Battle Born" appear on the Nevada state flag?

Because Nevada was admitted to the Union in 1864, during the Civil War. President Abraham Lincoln needed another Republican state to help support his antislavery policies in Congress. Even though Nevada didn't have the required number of people to form a state, people in Nevada went ahead and voted for statehood.

Why is Nevada called the Silver State?

Huge amounts of silver were mined in the 1800s in Nevada. The Comstock Lode, near Virginia City in the west-central part of the state, was the largest silver mining center ever in the United States. The dream of wealth drew thousands of people to Nevada from about 1860 until the late 1880s, when the silver began to run out and many of the settlements became ghost towns.

Today Nevada still has active silver mines. It could be called the Gold State because it produces about two-thirds of all the gold mined in the United States.

Nevada's scarce waters are home to several species of rare fish. They include the cui-ui, found only in Pyramid Lake, and the Devils Hole pupfish, found only in Devils Hole.

The U.S. government owns 85 percent of the land in Nevada, the highest percentage of any state.

Are California's redwood trees the oldest living things in the world?

No, but they are the tallest. One redwood tree in Redwood National Park is 368 feet (112 m) tall. One of the oldest living things in the world is in Sequoia National Park: the General Sherman Tree, a giant sequoia tree that is 272 feet (83 m) tall, has a circumference of 109 feet (33 m) at its base and is thought to be about 2,500 years old. But even older plants live in California: the bristlecone pine trees in California's White Mountains. Some are more than 4,000 years old. (See page 38 for more about the oldest living things.)

Where is Silicon Valley?

Silicon Valley is a 30-mile (48-km) by 10-mile (16-km) area in northern California between San Francisco and San Jose. Its name comes from the many electronics, information technology, and Internet companies that have been locating their offices and manufacturing plants there since the 1950s.

The term "Silicon Valley" was first used in 1971, with "silicon" referring to the material used to make computer chips. Close by are Stanford University and the University of California at Berkeley, which helped Silicon Valley develop into one of the world's most important research and development centers. Earlier in the twentieth century

Six U.S. state capitals lie west of Los Angeles, California: Honolulu, Hawaii; Juneau, Alaska; Salem, Oregon; Olympia, Washington; Sacramento, California; and Carson City, Nevada.

California's Number Ones

California is first in the nation in several ways. It has the most people—about 33 million, many more than Texas (20 million) and New York (18 million). It ranks number one among all the states in both manufacturing and agriculture. Cotton is the main crop, and dairy products and beef cattle are the primary farm products. If California was a country, it would rank as having the fifth-largest economy in the world.

California also is the home of two U.S. extremes in altitude: the highest point in the conterminous United States (Mount Whitney, 14,494 ft [4,418 m]) above sea level) and the lowest (Death Valley, 282 feet [86 m] below sea level).

this region was best known for its apricot and walnut orchards.

Why does San Francisco experience so much fog in the summertime?

When warm, humid air from the Pacific Ocean moves over the cooler water of San Francisco Bay it condenses, producing advection fog. This is the type of fog San Francisco experiences in the summer months, keeping the city cool, at least until it burns off around midday.

What was the worst earthquake to hit California in the twentieth century?

The 1906 San Francisco earthquake was the worst in the state's history, causing the deaths of more than 3,000 people and the destruction of 28,000 buildings. The fire that resulted made things worse, burning much of the city. Firefighters couldn't fight the fires because the earthquake caused the water pipes leading into the city to break.

The fault that ruptured as a result of the quake was the longest ever seen in the United States, extending from San Juan Batista to Point Arena, more than 186 miles (299 km). People were killed as far north of San Francisco as Santa Rosa, about 50 miles (80 km) away, and most people in California felt the quake.

Geologists rated this earthquake a XI on the modified Mercalli scale; on this scale, XII means total destruction. (See more about California earthquakes on page 41.)

How far is Hawaii from the California coast?

Honolulu, the capital of Hawaii, is about 2,400 miles (3,864 km) southwest of the U.S. mainland—about the same as the distance between San Francisco and Washington, D.C. It is the southernmost state in the Union—in fact, Honolulu is on about the same latitude as Guadalajara, Mexico.

Hawaii is the only U.S. state that is not part of the North American continent, and it is the only state made up of islands. It was the last state to join the Union, in 1959. Almost three-fourths of the people in Hawaii live on the island of Oahu.

Together, the states of California, Nevada, Utah, and Arizona are home to a fourth of all land plant species in the United States and Canada. The favorable climate in those states also lets farmers produce exotic fruits that are difficult to grow anywhere else in the country—for example, dates, olives, and kiwifruit.

The eight major Hawaiian islands are all volcanic in origin. Several volcanoes on the islands are active today.

How many islands make up the Hawaiian Islands chain?

Hawaii consists of 137 islands, most of which are very small and uninhabited. They spread over 6,423 square miles (16,700 sq km) of the North Pacific Ocean.

What are the names of the eight main Hawaiian islands?

Going from east to west, they are Hawaii, Maui, Kahoolawe, Lanai, Molokai, Oahu, Kauai, and Niihau. The Hawaiian Islands were once called the Sandwich Islands.

There are no other islands for thousands of miles around Hawaii. Why are they all by themselves?

The Hawaiian Islands are really the tips of ancient volcanoes. They owe their existence to their location over an unusual stationary "hot spot" deep within the Earth in this area. As the Pacific tectonic plate slowly moved northwestward over that hot spot, molten rock flowed through cracks in the Earth's surface and began to create—over a period of 70 million years—a long chain of volcanic islands.

Most of the volcanoes have been extinct for millions of years and lie below the sea. But the youngest volcanoes, on the Big Island of Hawaii, are still active. Kilauea, possibly the world's most active volcano, began erupting again in 1983 and has continued to this day. It first erupted perhaps as long as 600,000 years ago.

The Big Island is home to four other active volcanoes, including Mauna Loa, the largest on Earth. The last time it erupted was in 1984; between then and 1843, it erupted 33 times. The only other active Hawaiian volcano is Haleakala, on the island of Maui. It last erupted in 1790 and probably will erupt again someday.

Hawaii claims to have the wettest place on Earth: Mount Waialeale, on the island of Kauai, which receives an average annual rainfall of 460 inches (1,168 cm).

Why is Hawaii called the endangered species capital of the world?

The state of Hawaii has 316 species of plants and animals on the U.S. endangered species list—more than a third of the total list. The problem began a few hundred years ago when Polynesian and European settlers brought various kinds of plants and animals, such as dogs, chickens, pigs, rats, and mongooses there—animals that had never lived in Hawaii before. These animals killed many native species and destroyed their habitats, disrupting the natural balance. Human activity, such as cutting down forests to make way for homes and farms, also contributed to the destruction of natural habitats.

The Grand Canyon of the Pacific

The Hawaiian island of Kauai may be best known for its tropical gardens, but its dramatically beautiful Waimea canyon is the highlight of any visit there. Mark Twain once called this 10-mile (16-km)-long, 2-mile (3.2-km)-wide, and nearly 3,000-foot (914-m)-deep canyon the "Grand Canyon of the Pacific." Its red rock walls remind visitors of Arizona's Grand Canyon, but Waimea Canyon also features lush plant life, creating dramatic contrasts of red and green. The canyon was formed by the many streams cutting through rock on this rainy side of the island.

s Oregon mostly forest? ◆ Why do urban planners consider Portland, Oregon, to be a model city? ◆ Was Crater Lake in Oregon created by a meteor crashing to earth? ◆ What was the Oregon Trail? ◆ Why is the eastern part of Washington state so dry, and the western part so wet? ◆ Is Mount Rainier an active volcano? ◆ When did Mount St. Helens blow its top? ◆ How large is the Grand Coulee Dam in Washington State? ◆ How big is the in Puget Sound? ◆ What makes the Olympic Peninsula in western Washington state so unusual? ◆ How big is Alaska in comparison with other states? ◆ How far away is Alaska from the "lower 48" states? ◆ What was Seward's Folly? ◆ How

THE PACIFIC NORTHWEST

State and Capital	Name Origin	Nickname	State Bird	State Flower	Land Area in Square Miles (sq km)	2000 Population
Oregon (Salem)	From the French name for the Columbia River, Ouragan, meaning "hurricane"	Beaver State	Western meadow-lark	Oregon grape	96,981 (252,151)	3,421,399
Washington (Olympia)	For President George Washington	Evergreen State	Willow goldfinch	Coast rhododen-dron	68,192 (177,299)	5,894,121
Alaska (Juneau)	From Aleutian Indian word meaning "mainland"	Last Frontier	Willow ptarmigan	Forget-me-not	615,230 (1,599,598)	626,932

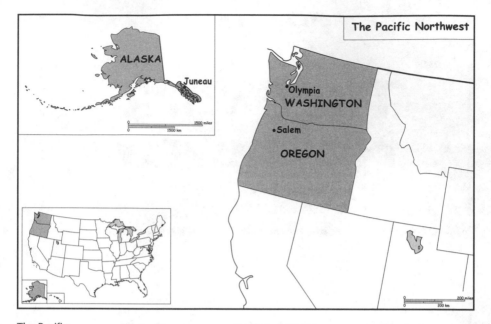

The Pacific Northwest

The Pacific Northwest states including capital cities. These states are marked by varied terrain not found in other parts of the United States—including tundra in Alaska and rainforests in Washington.

Is Oregon mostly forest?

Not quite—about half the state is covered with forests. Oregon leads the nation in lumber production, and it also is a big producer of plywood, veneer, and particleboard. The eastern part of the state is less forested, and farms there produce wheat and other grain crops as well as potatoes and other vegetables.

Why do urban planners consider Portland, Oregon, to be a model city?

Because Portland has been so successful in revitalizing its downtown area and limiting urban sprawl. (See more about urban sprawl on page 55.) Its light-rail transit system has reduced traffic congestion and air pollution, and coordinated land-use planning has kept the city from spreading uncontrolled into the surrounding countryside.

Unlike many U.S. cities, more people live and work in the downtown area now than 30 years ago. Almost half of Oregon's residents live in the Portland metropolitan area. The city lies along the Willamette River, close to where it joins the Columbia River.

Was Crater Lake in Oregon created by a meteor crashing to earth?

No. Crater Lake is the result of water collecting in the caldera, or crater, created by the volcanic eruption of Mount Mazama nearly 7,000 years ago. Crater Lake, which is in the Cascade Mountains, is the deepest lake in the United States, at 1,932 feet (589 m). It is 6 miles (9.7 km) wide. The first thing visitors notice about Crater Lake is its vivid blue color.

Almost all of the hazelnuts—also known as filberts—grown in the United States come from about 3.5 million hazelnut trees in Oregon's Willamette Valley.

What was the Oregon Trail?

This 2,000-mile (3,220-km) route through dangerous and rugged land was the "road" settlers took out of Independence, Missouri, to the Columbia River region of Oregon. The end of the trail was Oregon City, south of Portland. To go that distance in the mid-1800s took 4 to 6 months.

People heading to the Gold Rush in the 1840s took the southern part of the trail to California. The trail began in 1843 as a series of rivers and landmarks that people could follow, but it was easy to get lost, at least until the

The Oregon Trail stretched through many states in addition to Oregon. Its branches brought settlers from the east to Nevada, California, Utah, and Idaho as well.

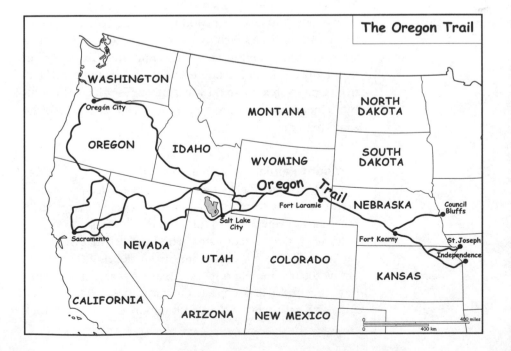

Portland, Oregon, was almost named Boston, Oregon. The town was founded in 1845 by two New England land developers—one from Boston, Massachusetts, the other from Portland, Maine. They flipped a coin to see whose hometown the new settlement would be named after.

paths were well worn enough to show the way. As many as 200,000 people may have followed the Oregon Trail to head west.

Before the Oregon Trail, the first Americans to reach the mouth of the Columbia River were the explorers Meriwether Lewis and William Clark, in 1805. Their expedition helped give the United States a claim to the land in the Pacific Northwest.

Why is the eastern part of Washington State so dry, and the western part so wet?

Weather on the western side of Washington is wet and quite warm, considering its northern latitude. For example, in January, on average, Seattle has a mean temperature of 41° Fahrenheit and receives 5 inches (12.7 cm) of rain. Spokane—just 282 miles (454 km) east and at about the same latitude—on average has a January temperature of 26° Fahrenheit and gets 1.8 inches (4.6 cm) of rain.

There are two reasons for this difference in climate. Western Washington lies next to the Pacific Ocean, which keeps it surrounded much of the year with warm, moist air. Second, the Cascades Mountain range blocks much of that moisture from reaching the eastern part of the state, a weather phenomenon called the rain shadow effect. In fact, before irrigation made eastern Washington a productive farming area, the land was almost desertlike. Oregon's two climatic regions are similar to Washington's, for the same reasons.

Is Mount Rainier an active volcano?

Yes, and geologists believe it is just a matter of time before some type of volcanic activity occurs there again. Some have even called Mount Rainier the most dangerous volcano in the United States. They predict that the worst threat to the area would come from debris flows, since about 100,000 people now live in areas where those flows have occurred in the past. Over the past 10,000 years, some 60 debris flows—a combination of mud and rock that slides down Mount Rainier's sides—have covered the surrounding region near Tacoma, Washington.

Located in the Cascade Mountain range, Mount Rainier covers 100 square miles (260 sq km) and is home to 41 glaciers. The last large eruption took place about 2,000 years ago, and the latest volcanic activity occurred in 1882. The U.S. Geological Survey constantly monitors volcanic activity at Mount Rainier and other volcanoes in the Cascades range.

Mount Rainier is the highest mountain in the state. On clear days it can be seen from Seattle, about 50 miles (81 km) away. This peak holds the record for the biggest snowfall ever recorded in one season in North America—from July 1971 through June 1972, the Rainier Paradise Ranger Station saw 1,122 inches (2,850 cm) of the white stuff.

When did Mount St. Helens blow its top?

Mount St. Helens, in the Cascades Mountains in Washington State, erupted for 6 days beginning on May 18, 1980. It immediately lost 1,314 feet (401 m) from its height and now stands at 8,363 feet (2,549 m). The eruption was triggered by an earthquake (5.1 on the Richter scale) 1 mile (1.6 km) below the volcano. Ash, lava, and debris from the eruption covered 231 square miles (601 sq km) of surrounding area, killing 57 people and more than 7,000 big-game animals such as deer, elk, and bear, not to mention countless fish, birds, and small mammals. The trees it destroyed would have provided enough lumber to build 300,000 two-bedroom houses.

Now, more than 20 years later, plants have begun to return to the area, mostly because large numbers of elk and deer are once more passing through the area, depositing plant seeds brought from elsewhere.

In addition, trees are growing around Mount St. Helens again. The U.S. Forest Service has planted 10 million trees on 14,000 acres (5,600 ha) of federal land in the area. Over the next 25 years the renewal process will continue, and the slopes of Mount St. Helens will be green once more.

Washington produces more apples and pears than any other state. Farmers in the central part of the state also grow much of the nation's berries, cherries, grapes, and plums.

There's a town in central Washington called George (population: 400), and its streets are named after varieties of cherries.

How large is the Grand Coulee Dam in Washington State?

It is 550 feet (168 m) tall and almost 1 mile (1.6 km) long, including the third powerhouse. Built of concrete on the Columbia River in the northeastern corner of the state, its three power plants generate more electricity than any other dam in the United States.

The Grand Coulee Dam also is the third-largest producer of electricity in the world. When construction began in 1933, the main purposes of the dam were to provide flood control and to irrigate farmland in the Columbia River Basin.

Today several smaller dams in the Pacific Northwest are under attack by environmental groups and Native American tribes, who want the dams removed because they have disrupted natural river flows, affecting the passage of fish, especially salmon.

How many islands are in Puget Sound?

About 170 islands make up the San Juan group. Puget Sound, in northwestern Washington State, is a Pacific Ocean inlet that runs through the state for about 100 miles, (161 km) from Whidbey Island south to Olympia, Washington.

Large ships can travel through the sound to several important port cities, including Seattle, Tacoma, Everett, and the Puget Sound Naval Shipyard in Bremerton.

What makes the Olympic Peninsula in western Washington state so unusual?

Three completely different ecosystems can be found there: dozens of glacier-capped mountains, 60 miles (97 km) of undeveloped Pacific coastline, and old-growth and temperate rain forests. Most of this region lies with the boundaries of Olympic National Park, 95 percent of which is designated as wilderness area. In addition, the region contains eight types of plants and five kinds of animals not found anywhere else in the world.

How big is Alaska in comparison with other states?

Alaska has 615,230 square miles (1,599,598 sq km). It is a fifth the size of all the lower 48 states put together, 2½

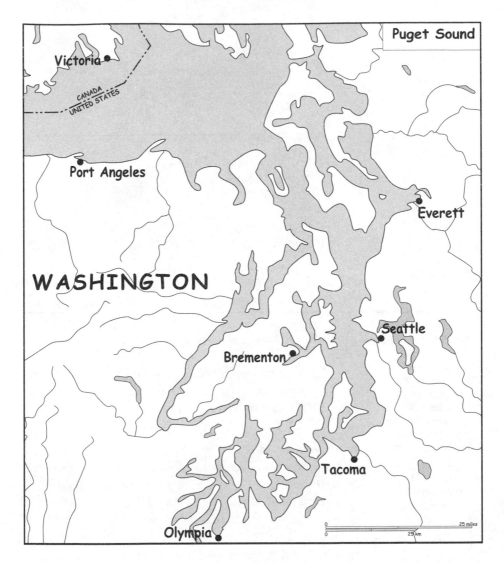

times bigger than Texas, and 488 times bigger than Rhode Island. In fact, just one glacier—the Malaspina, between Anchorage and Juneau—covers an area larger than Rhode Island.

How far away is Alaska from the "lower 48" states?

You'd have to travel across 500 miles (805 km) of Canada to get to the next closest U.S. state, Washington. Part of Alaska is actually much closer to Russia. Alaska's Little Diomede Island, at the extreme western end of the

Puget Sound is a large inlet of the Pacific Ocean that extends far into Washington State. Ecologically rich, the sound also provides shipping access to a number of western Washington cities.

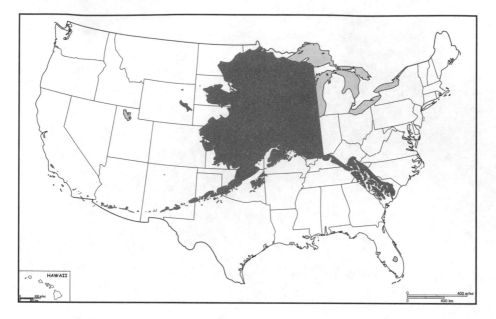

The area of Alaska is huge compared to the rest of the United States, but maps can make it hard to compare sizes accurately. This image shows Alaska and the conterminous United States to scale, showing just how big Alaska is compared to other states.

Seward Peninsula, is only 2.5 miles (4 km) from Big Diomede Island, which belongs to Russia.

Almost a third of Alaska lies within the Arctic Circle, but its northernmost point, at Point Barrow, is still 1,300 miles (2,093 km) from the North Pole.

What was Seward's Folly?

Seward's Folly refers to the U.S. purchase of Alaska from Russia. In 1867 the U.S. secretary of state, William H. Seward, offered to buy Alaska for $7.2 million—about 2 cents an acre—from the Russian government. Many Americans thought the idea was a waste of money, since they believed the land would prove to be worthless.

They were wrong; the state is full of valuable resources, particularly its oil reserves at Prudhoe Bay.

How bad was the Good Friday earthquake in Alaska?

In March 1964, the strongest earthquake in North America in the twentieth century hit central Alaska, in the area of Prince William Sound. It measured 8.5 on the Richter scale and lasted for 3 minutes, an enormous amount of time for an earthquake; most last less than a minute.

Many homes and buildings were destroyed by the quake and the landslides and tsunami that resulted, and 125 people were killed. The quake was felt all over Alaska as well as parts of Canada, and the tsunami caused damage as far away as Hawaii and the West Coast of the United States. (See page 44 for more about tsunami.)

Every year Alaska experiences about 5,000 earthquakes that measure at least 3.5 on the Richter scale. Three of the world's 10 worst earthquakes (and 8 of the United States' 10 worst) on record have occurred in Alaska.

Alaska is the only state in the Union that provides local government services through political units called boroughs, rather than counties. Boroughs collect taxes and otherwise work like counties, but in general they offer fewer services.

GLOSSARY

A

autonomous capable of existing or governing itself without outside control

B

bituminous coal sometimes called soft coal, bituminous is one of the two types of coal found in the earth. When heated, bituminous coal gives off large amounts of waste material potentially harmful for the environment. Anthracite, or hard coal, burns more efficiently than bituminous coal.

C

census a counting. National censuses of a country's population are periodically taken by the government.

confluence a meeting at one point

conterminous having a shared boundary

contiguous touching or connected at some point. The contiguous states do not include Hawaii and Alaska.

continent one of the seven principal divisions of land on Earth. The continents are North America, South America, Africa, Europe, Asia, Australia, and Antarctica.

country an independent political state or nation and its territories. A country has distinct boundaries, a government, a unique name, and a flag.

crag a sharp, rough rock

D

debris the scraps or remains of something destroyed

drought a shortage of water

E

eon in geology, a period of one billion years. In common terms, a period of time too long to measure.

epoch a period of time that contains a notable stage of development or series of events

equator the imaginary line of 0 degrees latitude that lies midway between the north and south poles

erosion the wearing away of structures, usually by water, wind, or ice

F

Fahrenheit the scale of measurement for temperature. Under standardized conditions, in the Fahrenheit system the boiling point of water is 212 degrees above 0 and the freezing point is 32 degrees above 0.

fossil fuels carbon-based fuels including coal, natural gas, and oil formed from the remains of animals and plants of the distant past

I

igneous type of rock and mineral produced by volcanic action

L

latitude the measure of distance north and south of the equator, from 0 degrees to 90 degrees north or south. Lines of latitude run east-west and are parallel to each other. Together, lines of latitude and *longitude* form a grid that lets us pinpoint exact locations on the Earth's surface.

longitude the angular distance east or west of the prime meridian, from 0 degrees to 180 degrees east or west. Lines of longitude run north-south. Together, lines of *latitude* and longitude form a grid that lets us pinpoint exact locations on the Earth's surface.

M

meteorology the science of the weather

mortality death

mountain a mass of land jutting up much higher than the surrounding area

N

northern hemisphere the half of the Earth that lies north of the equator, between 0 degrees (the equator) and 90 degrees north latitude (the North Pole).

P

per capita from the Latin "per head" referring to an amount counted per single person

plain a large area of land marked by an absence of trees and mainly level terrain

precipitation moisture that falls on the earth, such as rain, hail, mist, or snow

prime meridian the imaginary line denoting 0 degrees longitude that passes through the Royal Observatory in Greenwich, England

R

river a natural flow of water, usually of very large volume and extending for several miles; larger than a stream, often fed by several *tributaries*

rural describing open land, often used for agriculture and often lightly populated

S

sea level   the standard level of the surface of the sea. When the height of a mountain or land mass is measured "above sea level," it may extend underwater but is measured from the surface level of the water to its top.

sedimentary   referring to rock formed from the materials that sink to the bottom of a body of water, or matter that is deposited by water

seismograph   a machine used to measure the strength of an earthquake; a seismogram is the record of each movement in the earth

seismology   the science of earthquakes

T

topography   the structure of a piece of land; the graphic description of natural and man-made features and their structural relationship to one another in height and placement

tributary   a small stream feeding into a larger stream or lake

W

western hemisphere   the area occupied by the continents of North and South America and their surrounding waters that lies between 20 degrees west longitude and 160 degrees east longitude

SELECTED BIBLIOGRAPHY

Blobaum, Cindy, and Michael P. Kline (illustrator). *Geology Rocks!: 50 Hands-On Activities to Explore the Earth.* Charlotte, VT: Williamson Publishing, 1999.

De Blij, Harm. *Harm de Blij's Geography Book.* New York: John Wiley & Sons, Inc., 1995.

Decker, Robert, and Barbara Decker. *Volcanoes.* New York: W. H. Freeman & Co., 1997.

Demko, George, Jerome Agel, and Eugene Boe. *Why in the World: Adventures in Geography.* New York: Doubleday, 1992.

Fagan, Brian M. *The Great Journey: The Peopling of Ancient America.* New York: Thames and Hudson, 1989.

Frey, William H., Bill Abresch, and Jonathan Yeasting. *America by the Numbers: A Field Guide to the U.S. Population.* New York: New Press, 2001.

Gordon, Patricia, and Reed C. Snow. *Kids Learn America: Bringing Geography to Life with People, Places and History.* Charlotte, VT: Williamson Publishing Company, 1991.

Hilts, Len. *America: A Celebration of the United States.* New York: Rand McNally & Co., 1999.

Levy, Matthys. *Earthquake Games: Earthquakes and Volcanoes Explained by Games and Experiments.* New York: Margaret McElderry, 1997.

Ludlum, David M. *National Audubon Society Field Guide to North American Weather.* New York: Knopf, 1991.

Mattson, Mark T. *MacMillan Color Atlas of the United States.* New York: MacMillan Library Reference USA, 1996.

National Geographic Society, Special Publications Division. *Exploring Your World*. Washington, DC: National Geographic Society, 1993.

Pollock, Steve. *Eyewitness: Ecology*. New York: DK Publishing, 2000.

Stefoff, Rebecca. *The Young Oxford Companion to Maps and Mapmaking*. New York: Oxford University Press, 1995.

Watt, Fiona, Jeremy Gower, and Chris Shields. *Earthquakes and Volcanoes* (Usborne Understanding Geography). Tulsa, OK: EDC Publications, 1994.

Wright, David, and Jill Wright. *Facts on File Children's Atlas* (Facts on File Atlas Series). New York: Checkmark Books, 2000.

Wyckof, Jerome. *Reading the Earth: Landforms in the Making*. Mahwah, NJ: Adastra West, Inc., 1999.

THE NEW YORK PUBLIC LIBRARY'S RECOMMENDED READING LIST

Arnold, Caroline. *El Niño*. New York: Clarion Books, 1998.

The DK Geography of the World. New York: DK, 1996.

Falk, Randee. *Spotlight on the USA*. New York: Oxford University Press, 1993.

Heinrichs, Ann. *California*. New York: Children's Press, 1998.

———. *Pennsylvania*. New York: Children's Press, 2000.

Jenkins, Steve. *Hottest, Coldest, Highest, Deepest*. Boston: Houghton Mifflin, 1998.

Leacock, Elspeth. *Journeys in Time: A New Atlas of American History*. Boston: Houghton Mifflin, 2001.

McNair, Sylvia. *Rhode Island*. New York: Children's Press, 2000.

Malam, John. *Highest, Longest, Deepest: A Fold-Out Guide to the World's Record Breakers*. New York: Simon & Schuster Books for Young Readers, 1996.

Patent, Dorothy H. *Shaping the Earth*. New York: Clarion Books, 2000.

Perl, Lila. *It Happened in America: True Stories from the Fifty States*. New York: Henry Holt, 1992.

Sayre, April Pulley. *River and Stream*. New York: Twenty-First Century Books, 1996.

Shepherd, Donna W., *Alaska*. New York: Children's Press, 1999.

Simon, Seymour. *Mountains*. New York: Morrow Junior Books, 1994.

Williams, Jack. *The Weather Book*. 2nd ed. New York: Vintage Books, 1997.

INTERNET RESOURCES

Geography in General

www.nationalgeographic.com—Take the Geo-Bee Challenge on the kids' page, get the latest news on geographic events, find maps, and learn about places and people in the United States and around the world.

www.school.discovery.com/students—On this Discovery Channel site, go to the social studies section to find features and an online encyclopedia called "A–Z Geography."

www.infoplease.com—This almanac publisher offers facts and figures relating to U.S. geography.

www.geography.about.com—This site gives lots of information and links to other sites, covering many geographic topics.

The 50 States

www.globalcomputing.com/states.html—This site offers a shortcut to the official state government websites of all 50 states. Most of the sites provide information about the people, places, history, and products of the state.

Climate and Weather

www.nws.noaa.gov—This is the official site of the National Weather Service, providing the latest weather forecasts and historic weather data, plus much more weather-related information and links.

www.ncdc.noaa.gov—This site is run by the National Climatic Data Center of the National Oceanic and Atmospheric Administration (NOAA) and is a great source of information for U.S. and world weather data. Look in the "Contents" section for the section called "Climate Extremes and Weather Events" to find information on tornadoes, hurricanes, floods, and much more.

The Land and the Environment

www.epa.gov—This site belongs to the U.S. Environmental Protection Agency and gives information on air pollution, global warming, ecosystems, water pollution, and more.

www.usgs.gov—This is the huge official site of the U.S. Geological Survey. You can learn about earthquakes, volcanoes, hurricanes, floods, biology, water resources, mineral resources, geographic names, and much more, and it contains lots of maps and map information.

www.doi.gov/bureaus—This page, part of the U.S. Department of Interior website, gives links to its divisions: the National Park Service, the U.S. Fish and Wildlife Service, the Bureau of Indian Affairs, the Bureau of Land Management, and several other resources-related government agencies.

Energy

www.energy.gov—This is the official website of the U.S. Department of Energy, with information on energy efficiency, transportation, science and technology advances, and environmental quality.

Population Information

www.census.gov—Learn about the people of the United States, as revealed by the 2000 Census, as well as a minute-by-minute population clock of the United States and the world. The section called "State and Country Quick Facts" gives all sorts of statistics about people and businesses. The yearly *Statistical Abstract of the United States* is also available free online at this site; in the contents, it is listed under "Special Topics."

www.prb.org—This site, maintained by the Population Reference Bureau, a nonprofit organization, provides background, facts, and information on U.S. and world population.

INDEX

Page numbers in *italics* indicate maps.